Waltzing _with_ Bears

MANAGING RISK ON SOFTWARE PROJECTS

⌂DH *Also Available from Dorset House Publishing*

The Deadline: A Novel About Project Management
by Tom DeMarco
ISBN: 0-932633-39-0   Copyright ©1997   320 pages, softcover

Dr. Peeling's Principles of Management:
Practical Advice for the Front-Line Manager
by Nic Peeling
ISBN: 0-932633-54-4   Copyright ©2003   288 pages, softcover

More Secrets of Consulting: The Consultant's Tool Kit
by Gerald M. Weinberg
ISBN: 0-932633-52-8   Copyright ©2002   216 pages, softcover

Peopleware: Productive Projects and Teams, 2nd ed.
by Tom DeMarco and Timothy Lister
ISBN: 0-932633-43-9   Copyright ©1999   264 pages, softcover

Project Retrospectives: A Handbook for Team Reviews
by Norman L. Kerth   foreword by Gerald M. Weinberg
ISBN: 0-932633-44-7   Copyright ©2001   288 pages, softcover

The Psychology of Computer Programming: Silver Anniversary Edition
by Gerald M. Weinberg
ISBN: 0-932633-42-0   Copyright ©1998   360 pages, softcover

Quality Software Management, Vol. 4: Anticipating Change
by Gerald M. Weinberg
ISBN: 0-932633-32-3   Copyright ©1997   504 pages, hardcover

Why Does Software Cost So Much?
(And Other Puzzles of the Information Age)
by Tom DeMarco
ISBN: 0-932633-34-X   Copyright ©1995   248 pages, softcover

For More Information

✔ Contact us for prices, shipping options, availability, and more.

✔ Sign up for *DHQ: The Dorset House Quarterly* in print or PDF.

✔ Send e-mail to subscribe to *e-DHQ,* our e-mail newsletter.

✔ Visit Dorsethouse.com for excerpts, reviews, downloads, and more.

DORSET HOUSE PUBLISHING
An Independent Publisher of Books on
Systems and Software Development and Management. Since 1984.
353 West 12th Street   New York, NY 10014   USA
1-800-DH-BOOKS   1-800-342-6657
212-620-4053   fax: 212-727-1044
info@dorsethouse.com   www.dorsethouse.com

Waltzing *with* Bears

MANAGING RISK ON SOFTWARE PROJECTS

TOM DEMARCO & TIMOTHY LISTER

Dorset House Publishing
353 West 12th Street
New York, NY 10014

Library of Congress Cataloging-in-Publication Data

DeMarco, Tom.
  Waltzing with bears : managing risk on software projects / Tom DeMarco
& Timothy Lister.
      p. cm.
Includes bibliographical references and index.
  ISBN 0-932633-60-9 (soft cover)
  1. Computer software--Development--Management. 2. Risk management.
I. Lister, Timothy R. II. Title.
  QA76.76.D47D4755 2003
  005.1'068--dc21

                                                    2003043481

Trademark credits: All trade and product names are either trademarks, registered trademarks, or service marks of their respective companies, and are the property of their respective holders and should be treated as such.

Cover Illustration: Tom DeMarco, detail from "Beach Dreams"
Author Photograph: James Robertson
Cover Design: David W. McClintock

Distributed in the English language in Singapore, the Philippines, and Southeast Asia by Alkem Company (S) Pte. Ltd., Singapore; in the English language in India, Bangladesh, Sri Lanka, Nepal, and Mauritius by Prism Books Pvt., Ltd., Bangalore, India; and in the English language in Japan by Toppan Co., Ltd., Tokyo, Japan.

Printed in the United States of America

Library of Congress Catalog Number: 2003043481

ISBN: 0-932633-60-9   12   11   10   9   8   7   6   5   4   3   2

ACKNOWLEDGMENTS

Many people believe that the roles of editor and publisher consist of checking spelling and grammar and overseeing the printing process. No. We thank David McClintock, Wendy Eakin, Vincent Au, and Nuno Andrade of Dorset House for their work taking our manuscript and molding it, transforming it, and coaxing it into a book we two are very proud of. The "before and after pictures" are remarkable. Thank you.

We also want to thank our colleagues who have generously jumped at the chance to give us their opinions and insights pro bono. It is just these conversations that give us the joy of working in our profession. Our thanks go to Rob Austin, Barry Boehm, Christine Davis, Mike Evans, Sean Jackson, Steve McMenamin, and Mike Silves.

We especially thank Bob Charette and the late Paul Rook for trailblazing this area. Our path has been much easier to follow thanks to them.

Finally, we thank our consulting clients of the last ten years. These are the companies that demonstrated to us that running away from risk is a loser, and that risk comes with the territory of a valuable project. We recognize that these people are not afraid to work on risky efforts; they want to work on important ventures.

To Sally O. Smyth and Wendy Lister
Risk Managers Extraordinaire

AUTHORS' NOTE

This text is divided into five parts, each one intended to answer one of the major questions likely to be on the mind of a new or potential risk manager:

Part I: Why bother to do risk management?
Part II: Why shouldn't we do it? (Wherein the authors come clean about some of the potential negatives of introducing risk management into an organization that isn't quite ready for it.)
Part III: How shall we go about it?
Part IV: How much risk should our organization be willing to take?
Part V: How do we know whether or not our risk management approach is working?

The page introducing each new part breaks down the overall question into detailed questions. By reading the chapters in each part, you should find answers to all those questions—or we haven't done our job.

Voice

Most of the text is written in the plural voice, with "we" standing for both authors. On occasion, we like to get in a word or two in our individual voices, and that gives rise to paragraphs set off like these:

TRL: Here's me (Tim) speaking in my own voice.

TDM: And this one is me (Tom).

Website

As we mention later, in Chapter 12, we've built a Website to complement the text. You'll find it at

http://www.systemsguild.com/riskology

We have placed some tools there to help your risk management effort, and we will endeavor to keep the site updated as we learn about new risk management tools or news on the subject.

Our Title

Our title is taken from a song included in *The Cat in the Hat Songbook,* by Dr. Seuss.[1] The song tells of Uncle Terwilliger, who every Saturday night "creeps down our back stairs,/sneaks out of our house to go waltzing with bears."

Uncle T. is a willing risk taker—we can only hope that he has a workable understanding of risk assessment, containment, and mitigation. If so, he is a perfect model for managers of risky software projects, people who may need to dance on occasion with a few bears of their own.

---

[1]Dr. Seuss and Eugene Poddany, *The Cat in the Hat Songbook* (New York: Random House, 1967).

CONTENTS

Waltzing *with* Bears

MANAGING RISK ON SOFTWARE PROJECTS

PROLOGUE

THE ETHICS OF BELIEF

L ondon, April 11, 1876: The scene is Grosvenor Square, just
before 10 P.M. Around us, on the sidewalks of the square,
Victorian gentlemen, many in top hats and evening clothes, are
making their way toward the ornate entrance of the Grosvenor
Hotel. We follow them in and are guided toward the upstairs
parlor, where the monthly meeting of London's elite
Metaphysical Society is to take place.

The Society's members include Alfred Tennyson, William
Gladstone, Thomas Huxley, Cardinal Manning, Arthur James
Balfour . . . in short, the cream of London intelligentsia. The subject this evening is, as always, philosophy. Before the proceed-
ings begin, the participants are talking in small groups, picking up
threads of the last meeting's discussion. As we wander among
these clusters, we hear such terms as ontology, tautology, and
epistemology. Some of the discussions are heated.

There is a certain tension in the room this evening, due to
the selection of the meeting's featured speaker. He is the
Society's newest member, William Kingdon Clifford. Clifford is
a professor of logic and mathematics at London's University
College. He is considered an iconoclast, possibly an atheist, and
is known to be a fiery debater. With his selection, he has become
the youngest person ever accepted into the Society.

By convention, each new member must prepare a paper and
read it to the membership at his first meeting. Only the title of

Clifford's paper, "The Ethics of Belief," has been made public, not the paper's contents. It promises to be a stunner.

Indeed, before Clifford has even finished reading, half the room has stomped out in angry protest. The Society's Secretary has publicly resigned; it would have been his job to arrange a private printing of the paper, and this he has refused to do. The remaining members are on their feet, either cheering Clifford on or trying to shout him down. The temperature in the room has shot up markedly and the entire scene is, well, a bit *un-British*.

What was it about "The Ethics of Belief" that got the members so hot? In the essay, Clifford asserts that what you choose to believe ought not to be exempt from the ethical judgment of others. Your belief may open you to a charge of unethical behavior, depending on whether, in Clifford's words, you have "a right to believe" the thing that you believe.[1]

He offers as an example the owner of an emigrant ship that is about to set sail with a full complement of passengers. The owner is bothered by worries that the ship is old and in poor condition and wasn't built very well in the first place. There is a real question in his mind about whether it can safely make another passage. With a bit of effort, though, the shipowner overcomes his doubts and persuades himself that no great harm will come from just one more passage. The ship, after all, has weathered more than a few storms in its day and always managed to limp home to port. Why not one more time?

The ship puts to sea and is lost with all hands.

"What shall we say of the owner?" Clifford asks, and gives his own answer:

> *Surely this, that he was verily guilty of the death of those men. It is admitted that he did sincerely believe in the soundness of his ship; but the sincerity of his conviction can in no wise help him, because he had no right to believe on such evidence as was before him. He had acquired his belief not by honestly earning it in patient investigation, but by stifling his doubts. And although in the end he may have felt so sure about it that he could not think otherwise, yet inasmuch as he had knowingly and willingly worked himself into that frame of mind, he must be held responsible for it.*

---

[1] See Appendix A for Part 1 of "The Ethics of Belief."

Clifford then goes back over the same story and alters it slightly. Suppose, he tells us, that the ship had managed after all to complete the voyage with no loss of life. Would the owner have been less guilty?

> *Not one jot. When an action is once done, it is right or wrong forever; no accidental failure of its good or evil fruits can possibly alter that. The man would not have been innocent, he would only have been not found out. The question of right or wrong has to do with the origin of his belief, not the matter of it; not what it was, but how he got it; not whether it turned out to be true or false, but whether he had a right to believe on such evidence as was before him.*

Prior to Clifford, there was a presumption that your beliefs could never be considered in an ethical light. You could believe any damn thing you pleased. You could even believe impossible things, as the White Queen did in *Through the Looking Glass.* When Alice protests that one simply cannot believe impossible things, the Queen responds,

> *"I daresay you haven't had much practice. . . . When I was your age, I always did it for half-an-hour a day. Why, sometimes I've believed as many as six impossible things before breakfast."*

There is probably no job on earth for which an ability to believe six impossible things before breakfast is more of a requirement than software project management. We are routinely expected to work ourselves into a state of believing in a deadline, a budget, or a performance factor that time subsequently may prove to be impossible.

We do this in a process that's not so terribly different from when the shipowner talked himself into believing in his ship. You have almost certainly been through this process yourself one or more times. There may have been others, egging you on. Your boss, for example, asks you to consider taking on a project that has to be done by Christmas, with only three people available to work on it. You express doubts that there is enough time to get the software built.

"That's why I picked *you* to manage the job," your boss tells you, confidently.

The fix is in: You'll get the job, the challenge, and the prestige . . . but you'll have to believe in the schedule. That's the price you pay. You swallow hard and say you'll do it. Later, you bolster your belief. Sure, why not Christmas? Other projects have accomplished as much in as little time, haven't they? Before long, you may find yourself actually feeling confident. Time may prove otherwise, but for the moment, you are practically sure you can get the job done.

At that moment, though, William Kingdon Clifford's question should be coming back to haunt you. Yes, that's what you believed, *but did you have any right to believe it?* Did you have a right to believe in that schedule, based on the evidence that was before you?

The business of believing only what you have a right to believe is called *risk management*. This essential discipline applies Clifford's ethics of belief to any effort that is complicated by elements of uncertainty. It will guide you through that effort (a software project, for example) in a way that eliminates the fabric of little lies and self-deceptions that have so hampered your work in the past. It will become your alternative to believing "six impossible things before breakfast."

PART I

WHY

- Why manage risk—why not simply avoid it?
- What is a risk, and what is risk management?
- What are the consequences of unmanaged risk?
- Isn't good process enough to take care of risks?
- Why do we need a new discipline?

1

RUNNING TOWARD RISK

Running away from risk is a no-win proposition. Sometimes, you come across a project that looks positively risk-free. In the past, you may have looked at such an endeavor as a slam dunk and thanked your lucky stars to be given an easy project for a change. We've had the same reaction. What dummies we were. Projects with no real risks are losers. They are almost always devoid of benefit; that's why they weren't done years ago. Save yourself some time and energy and apply it to something worthwhile:

> If a project has no risks, don't do it.

Risks and benefits always go hand in hand. The reason that a project is full of risk is that it leads you into uncharted waters. It stretches your capability, which means that if you pull it off successfully, it's going to drive your competition batty. The ultimate coup is to stretch your own capability to a point beyond the competition's ability to respond. This is what gives you competitive advantage and helps you build a distinct brand in the market.

Flight from Opportunity

Companies that run away from risk and focus on what they know they can do well are ceding the field to their adversaries. The 1990's gave us some charming examples of this. There were, broadly speaking, two major things going on in the nineties:

1. Companies were moving applications and databases from the old mainframe-and-terminal mode to client/server mode.
2. Companies were transforming themselves to interact directly with their customers and suppliers in new and previously unimagined ways: via the Internet and through integrated supply chains, auction mechanisms, and disintermediated transactions.

Unfortunately, there were lots of companies that dedicated themselves substantially to the first of these and ignored the second. Once you've done one client/server conversion, the rest are easy and mechanical. You could do them in your sleep. In fact, if you spent most of the nineties doing client/server conversions, you *were* asleep. You missed the action.

A case in point is Merrill Lynch. It looked long and hard at the so-called trend of on-line trading . . . and decided to ignore it. It crossed its fingers in the hope that the era of the full-service brokerage (with fat fees and brokers who could keep you endlessly on hold) would come back, that direct trading would be only a passing fad. What a forlorn hope. Today, the full-service brokerage is as much a thing of the past as the full-service gas station. And today, Merrill Lynch offers its customers on-line trading at a reduced fee. But it took the company nearly a decade to catch on. Merrill Lynch was the latest of the Late Adopters.

The Early Adopters were Fidelity, Schwab, and E-Trade. E-Trade and its look-alikes were new companies, created to exploit the change. So, if on-line trading had turned out to be only a passing fad, E-Trade would have gone belly-up with no loss beyond the capital the company had raised explicitly to put at risk. Fidelity and Schwab, on the other hand, were well-established companies with a lot to lose. In this sense, they were not so different from Merrill Lynch. But Fidelity and Schwab were willing to take the risks.

The IT people at Fidelity and Schwab had to be aware of the risks of the new venture. Here is our two-minute brainstorm list of the risks that would have been easily apparent to Fidelity and Schwab when they began to take on Web trading in the early nineties:

- Building the system is completely beyond our capability; we'll have to learn protocols, languages, and approaches like HTML, Java, PERL, CGI, server-side logic, verification, secure Web pages, and many new technologies that we can't even name today.
- Supporting the system is completely beyond our present capability; we'll have to set up user help desks, audit trails, monitoring software, tutorials for use of the system—things that we've never done before.
- The security risks of on-line trading are truly daunting; we will be attacked by hackers and crackers, by organized crime, and by our own customers and employees.
- We may not be able to acquire the experience and talent we need to do any of this.
- We may find that the business we do via the Web is just what we would have done with the same customers at higher fees if we hadn't built the Web trading system.
- We may find that people try on-line trading and then go back to telephone trading, leaving us with a busted investment.
- We may case our existing customers into this new mode and then lose them to competitors that cater to these newly savvy traders.

Undoubtedly, Merrill Lynch was aware of the same risks. But Fidelity and Schwab decided to run directly toward those risks, while Merrill Lynch chose to run away from them. The result was that Fidelity and Schwab grew aggressively in the nineties while Merrill Lynch struggled to stay even.

What's Different About Today?

We are in the midst of a sea change that will probably cause turmoil for the rest of our lives. The world is suddenly much more tightly connected. There is an ever broader-band web of digital connection that touches all of us: Individuals are more connected to each other, to their companies, and to the service providers that they depend upon; companies are more connected to their clients and employees, to their markets, to their vendors, and to the government agencies that affect their work. And all of this is still evolving.

In this period of turmoil, a willingness to run risks is utterly essential. It matters a hell of a lot more than efficiency. Efficiency will make you, at best, an attractive takeover candidate—probably for a less-efficient competitor that has stolen a march on you through greater risk-taking.

Charette's Risk Escalator

Author and risk management expert Bob Charette has proposed a useful new way to think about risk-taking in today's environment. He asks you to imagine your company and its competitors as a set of down escalators. You are obliged to climb up your escalator, which is moving against you. And your competitors are doing the same thing on theirs. The faster the stairs move, the faster everyone has to climb to stay even. If you pause, even for a moment, you begin to fall behind. And, of course, if you pause for too long, you will drop off the bottom, no longer able to compete.

New competitors in Charette's perverse escalator world get to enter their escalators halfway up. Falling behind, then, guarantees that new competition will enter above you.

At the top of each escalator is a lever that will allow you to control the speed of not just your escalator, but of everyone else's as well. If you're the first to reach the lever, that shows that you're a better climber than your competitors. So, you can speed up all the stairs so that you can stay even but your competitors cannot.

It's the risks that you take that speed up the stairs for everyone else. Not taking them just assures that your world will come to be shaped and dominated by someone else. This is an era in which risk-taking is rewarded, leaving companies that run away from risk as plunder to be divided up by the others.

Ignoring Risk

Companies that seem to understand the necessity of risk-taking are sometimes prone to the following strange behavior: They try to emphasize positive thinking by ignoring the possible unfortunate consequences of the risk they're taking. This is an extreme variant of the can-do attitude. After all, risk awareness involves at least a bit of *can't-do* thinking, they reason, so it can't be good. In order to stay positive, they steadfastly refuse to consider much of the downside. If there are things that could go wrong, that would make your project a total fiasco, for example, they would just have you not think about those things at all.

Now, nobody is so stupid as to ignore *all* risk. When people do this dumb thing, ignoring risk, they do it selectively. The way it typically works is, they take elaborate care to list and analyze and monitor all the minor risks (the ones they can hope to counteract through managerial action) and only ignore the really ugly ones.

TDM: *As a member of the Airlie Council, a Department of Defense (DoD) advisory group overseeing government software acquisition practices, I sometimes sit in on risk management briefings. I was particularly interested to see how one project that I'd been following from afar would deal with what I viewed as a truly daunting risk. Because it was building software to replace a Y2K non-compliant system, late delivery would be a real disaster. And I had heard that the code to be delivered was nearly six times larger than anything the contractor had ever been able to build in the time allocated for the project. The daunting risk was that the project would be late and leave the organization with no workable alternatives.*

When the project manager produced a list of his key risks, I was surprised to find that not one of them had to do with schedule. In fact, the major risk in his estimate was "PC performance," the fear that the current configuration would not have enough horsepower. "But hey, don't worry about that one," he told us. "We have a plan for that, a beefed-up configuration." I quickly came to understand that if he didn't have a plan for how to counteract a risk, then he ignored it.

This is hardly a formula for sensible risk management. If you're going to run toward risk instead of away from it, you need to keep both eyes open and firmly focused on what's ahead.

Now What?

Our intention in this initial chapter is to make a case for risk-taking in general (the strategy of running toward risk, rather than away from it). We also wanted to dangle just enough of our philosophy of risk management in front of you to raise a few issues. Following are some of the questions that might be on your mind at this point, questions we'll address in the chapters and parts ahead:

- What exactly is a risk and what does it mean to manage it? (Chapter 2)
- What are the consequences of unmanaged risk? (Chapter 3)
- Why bother to invest in a different approach? (Chapter 4)
- What problems do I incur by doing risk management? (Part II)
- How do I go about it? (Part III)
- How do I achieve a balance of risk and opportunity? (Part IV)
- How do I know whether or not I have succeeded? (Part V)

2

RISK MANAGEMENT IS PROJECT MANAGEMENT FOR ADULTS

Team Leader:	*We're having a meeting about this tomorrow, but I think it will get worse.*
Project Manager:	*Don't have the meeting.*

This chapter of definitions pertinent to risk management begins with a definition (right in the title) of risk management itself: project management for adults.

This is not meant to be snide. (Okay, it's meant to be a little snide, but there is also truth in it.) An almost-defining characteristic of adulthood is a willingness to confront the unpleasantness of life, from the niggling to the cataclysmic. A little child is excused from thinking about nuclear war, the rape of the environment, kidnapping, heartless exploitation, and rampant injustice. But as that child's parent, you are obliged to keep such matters in your mind, at least enough to make sure that the child's temporary ignorance of them doesn't lead to tragedy. You have to face up to unpleasant realities. That's what it means to be a grown-up.

Taking explicit note of bad things that can happen (risks) and planning for them accordingly is a mark of maturity. But that's not the way we tend to use the word *maturity* in the IT industry. We software people tend to equate maturity with technical proficiency. We even have a five-level scheme for measuring such maturity, the Capability Maturity Model (CMM).[1]

---

[1]All we need now is a twelve-step program to help us wean ourselves from measuring maturity in a five-level scheme.

But the word *maturity* in standard English has nothing to do with technical proficiency. It is, rather, a quality of grown-up-ness, an indication that a person or organism has reached its adult state.

In retrospect, when we as project managers did not explicitly manage our risks, we were being childlike. Our whole industry has been childlike in this respect. Our infatuation with positive thinking and a can-do attitude has fixated us on the best outcomes as we ignored the various realities that could make such outcomes impossible. (See in particular the case study in Chapter 3 for an example of this.)

Considering only the rosy scenario and building it into the project plan is real kid stuff. Yet we do that all the time. While we've been doing these immature things, we've been positively trumpeting our increased "maturity" due to improvements in our technical proficiency.

What's needed now is maturity in the other, more traditional, sense. We need to grow up, take explicit note of our risks, and plan accordingly. That's what risk management is all about.

But all of this has put the cart slightly before the horse, defining risk management without first defining the component word, *risk*. So, what is a risk?

Risk: The Temporary Definition

Our concept of risk in software projects is derived from watching numbers of such projects go awry. Much of our consulting work these days is supporting litigation, the aftermath of projects that came a cropper. This has helped us compile an extensive set of data points about failure. The risks of those failed projects, in retrospect, were the factors that led to the undesirable outcomes. So, too, for future projects: Their risks are the things that *might* lead to an undesirable outcome. That leads us to the following temporary definition of risk:

> **risk** *n 1: a* possible *future event that will lead to an undesirable outcome 2: the undesirable outcome itself*

The first of these is the cause and the second is the effect. Both are important, but don't gull yourself into thinking that you can manage both. The business of risk management is all about managing the causal risks. Those are the ones you *can* manage. (The justification for risk management in the first place, however, is all about the outcomes.)

Our definition is a temporary one because it assumes a binary character to each risk, treating it as something that can either happen or not. There are, of course, many risks that don't work this way; they occur partially and have a proportional adverse effect on the project. To take account of these nonbinary risks, we shall have to revisit this definition in a later chapter. For now, though, the temporary definition will serve us well.

Risks and Problems

As an alternative, consider the following circular definition of risk: A *risk* is a problem that has yet to occur, and a *problem* is a risk that has already materialized.

Before it happens, a risk is just an abstraction. It's something that *may* affect your project, but it also may not. There is a possibility that ignoring it will not come back to bite you. Even so, you're not innocent of management malpractice for not having considered the risk. In William Clifford's words, you're just— "not found out."

Risk management is the process of thinking out corrective actions before a problem occurs, while it's still an abstraction. The opposite of risk management is *crisis management,* trying to figure out what to do about the problem after it happens.

Risk Transitions and Transition Indicators

Imagine the moment when something that used to be a risk suddenly becomes a problem. It used to be an abstraction, a mere possibility, and now it is not abstract at all. It has happened. This is the point at which the risk is said to *materialize.* It is the moment of *risk transition.*

Transition is a key concept for the risk manager—it is the triggering event for whatever is planned to deal with the risk. Well, almost. The actual transition may be invisible to you (for example, Saddam Hussein decides to invade Kuwait). What you do see is a *transition indicator* (the massing of troops at the border). For every risk you need to manage, there is some kind of transition indicator. Some indicators are more useful than others, though. More about that in a moment.

Mitigation

The reason you care about the transition is that when the indicator fires, you intend to take some action. Before the transition, it's too early to take the action—it may be expensive and time-consuming—so you are justified in hoping that it won't be necessary. However, while you may be able to defer some of the corrective action, other parts may not be deferrable. There may be some steps you have to take before the transition, in order to keep your options open and to make correction possible afterward. That work is called *mitigation.*

Consider an example of mitigation from a domain outside our own: the U.S. court system. Realizing that a juror might become sick, drop out, die, or become otherwise unfit to continue, the courts appoint a number of alternate jurors to each jury case. If the original slate is able to finish, the alternates have no role; if a spare juror is required, however, an alternate—fully versed in the proceeding by virtue of having been present throughout—steps in and completes the requirement for a full jury. The risk here is the loss of a juror, leading to an aborted case, a retrial, and all the attendant expense and delay. The mitigating action is to carry one or more alternate jurors from day one. If and when the risk materializes, it can be contained at minimal cost.

The IT project analog to loss of a juror is personnel turnover, one of the core risks on all software projects. And the counterpart to appointment of alternate jurors would be to overstaff slightly from the beginning, with the fully qualified extra hands temporarily filling apprentice and support roles. When turnover occurs, the manager doesn't have to hire new staff. One of the extras can move up from the apprentice role to assume the duties of the person departing, with minimal time lost to ramp-up.

Mitigation costs both time and money. Yet in the rosiest of rosy scenarios, that expenditure of time and money turns out to have been unnecessary. We'll come back to this point, because it leads to a kind of pathology that can make risk management virtually impossible.

Example: Risk Management in a School

For some exercise in the use of all of these newly defined terms, imagine yourself practicing risk management in a school.

Suppose that you are principal of the operation, a glitzy private boarding school for boys and girls in grades 5 through 8.

Since you are a professional in your field, you are well aware that there are certain awful things (risks) that might happen to the children left in your care. You don't just think about these matters from time to time; they are on your mind constantly. After all, these are *other people's children* you're looking out for, and you can't take that responsibility lightly.

Some of the bad things that might happen can be safely handled by you and your staff with nothing more than a little quick thinking at the moment of transition. For example, there is no need to have an elaborate plan in place for how to deal with a pillow fight. Any teacher worth his or her salt will figure out how to handle that one and act accordingly.

But, you realize, there is a class of graver risks that require you to have done at least some serious planning in advance. Fire in one of the dorms, for example, is such a risk. You would be disgraced should it be proved after a fire that you hadn't done certain homework before the fire broke out. The homework (mitigation) needed before the event includes the placement of fire extinguishers, the installation of alarms, fire drills, an investment in sprinklers, and so forth.

The actual occurrence (transition) of this particular risk will probably be invisible to you when it happens, so you have to put in place and monitor some kind of mechanism (transition indicator) to spot it when it begins. You have a choice of several mechanisms. You might just ask the janitor to take a moment every few hours to poke about the facility looking for smoke or flame. Or you might install smoke alarms. In making your choice, you decide that you should try for the earliest practical indicator of the transition, so the smoke alarm is clearly preferable.

Realizing that fire is only one of the risks requiring advance homework, you call together your teachers and staff and pose the problem to them. You suggest, Let's have an exploratory session (a risk-discovery brainstorm), and make up a definitive list (a risk census) of all the risks for which advance preparation is needed.

"What are the risks requiring advance preparation?" you ask them. They call out such things as fire, sports injury, food-poisoning, sexual abuse by a teacher or staff member or outside stranger, sexual experimentation by students, drugs, guns, depression leading to suicide, attacks on teachers or children, and so on.

Included among the suggestions are some that aren't worth managing ("meteor hits school and blows it to smithereens with loss of all staff and students"). There are others for which the extent of your responsibility is not so obvious. For example, "some aspect of a science lesson shakes a student's religious faith." Is this a risk you need to manage? You note it down and press on with the brainstorm. Afterward, you're going to have to go back over the list and do some further work on the risks (risk analysis). You'll have to decide which ones to manage and which ones not (risk triage). For those you elect to manage, you will need, at the very least, to figure out your best trigger (transition indicator), plan your pretransition actions (mitigation), and assess the relative importance of the risk (exposure analysis).

When the brainstorm bogs down, that doesn't mean you're done. You will want to put some kind of persistent mechanism in place (an ongoing risk-discovery process) to pick up new risks that require management. You may want to appoint one person to be especially responsible for this (a risk officer).

Component Activities of Risk Management

Abstracting backward from this single example, we see five main activities that make up the practice of risk management:

- *risk discovery:* your initial risk brainstorm and subsequent triage, plus whatever mechanism you put in place to keep the process going
- *exposure analysis:* quantification of each risk in terms of its probability of materializing and its potential impact
- *contingency planning:* what you expect to do if and when the risk materializes
- *mitigation:* steps that must be taken before transition in order to make the planned contingency actions possible and effective when required
- *ongoing transition monitoring:* tracking of managed risks, looking for materialization

The first of these is an overall activity, while all the others are done on a per-risk basis.

Once More Over the Same Ground

Risk management is something that most of us practice all the time—everywhere except the office. In our personal lives, we face up to such risks as sickness and early death. We mitigate by buying life and health insurance and by making arrangements for who will look out for the kids if something bad happens. We don't pretend to be immortal or that our earning capacity can never be harmed by bad luck. Each time we take on a new responsibility—say, a mortgage—we go over all the awful things that we hope won't happen and force ourselves to think, What if they do?

Risk management is not rocket science. But as we'll see, practicing it in the office involves a few special challenges.

The Special Challenge of Unthinkable Risk

Some of the risks confronting a project may be fatal. By this, we mean fatal to the hopes and aspirations of those who engendered the project in the first place. These risks are the most essential to manage, but managing them sensibly may bring you into conflict with established cultural norms. Your project may have been placed on a fixed schedule by the CEO's public announcement—carried in all the press—that the product would be delivered on a certain date. By going very public with the date, the CEO has attempted to make schedule slip unthinkable.

Declaring an unwanted outcome unthinkable does not make it impossible, as we all know. But it may make risk management nearly impossible. Consider the example in the very next chapter. . . .

3

DENVER INTERNATIONAL
AIRPORT RECONSIDERED

The city of Denver, Colorado, set out in 1988 to build a new air-port to replace the existing one, Stapleton Airport. Stapleton was judged incapable of expansion, inadequate to serve the growing city, and guilty of contributing to ever-more-evident noise- and air-pollution problems. With the new airport, costs would be reduced, pollution and air-traffic delays would be eliminated, and growth would be assured. The new Denver International Airport (DIA) was scheduled to open on October 31, 1993. That was the plan.

Another Fine Mess

Cut to the chase: Everything went fine, except those damn software guys let the side down again. (Sigh, groan, general rolling of the eyes.) On October 31, 1993, every other part of the vast airport complex was ready to go . . . honest it was. Really. Trust us on this. But the software wasn't ready, so the airport couldn't open!

Specifically, what wasn't ready on time was the infamous DIA Automated Baggage Handling System (ABHS). The airport couldn't open without functional baggage-handling software. Since building the airport involved huge capital expenditure, all that capital was tied up while the software guys scrambled around playing catch up. And

time is money. The taxpayers took the hit. This is not a matter subject to elaborate analysis; it is as simple as this:

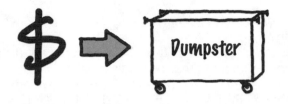

And it was all the fault of those awful software people.

   This kind of dollars-to-dumpster simplification was a fea-
ture of newspaper and journal coverage of the DIA troubles from
the first sign of delay in early 1993 until the partial opening in
1995. So much blame was laid on the software team that even
today, the phrase "DIA Automated Baggage Handling System" is
a recognized symbol of incompetent software projects.

   An article in *Scientific American* put responsibility for the
DIA disappointment squarely on the software industry and its lax
standards and practices:

> *software engineering discipline remains years—per-
> haps decades—short of the mature engineering dis-
> cipline needed to meet the demands of an informa-
> tion-age society.*[1]

This was a process problem, the article asserted. The delays at
DIA might very well have been avoided, the article claimed, if
only the project had improved its process to include

1. higher CMM level
2. more use of formal methods
3. mathematical specification languages like B and VDM

But was it really a process problem?

Beyond the Process

Suppose you had an utterly perfect process for delivering software. Would that remove all uncertainty from your projects? In

---

[1]W. Wayt Gibbs, "Software's Chronic Crisis," *Scientific American* (September
1994), p. 84.

fact, is the software building process even one of the *major* sources of uncertainty? We suggest not. Among the more important sources of uncertainty are these:

1. *Requirement:* What exactly is it that the system has to do?
2. *Match:* How will the system interact with its human operators and other peer systems?
3. *Changing environment:* How will needs and goals change during the period of development?
4. *Resources:* What key human skills will be available (when needed) as the project proceeds?
5. *Management:* Will management have sufficient talent to set up productive teams, maintain morale, keep turnover low, and coordinate complex sets of interrelated tasks?
6. *Supply chain:* Will other parties to the development perform as hoped?
7. *Politics:* What is the effect of using political power to trump reality and impose constraints that are inconsistent with end-project success?
8. *Conflict:* How do members of a diverse stakeholder community resolve their mutually incompatible goals?
9. *Innovation:* How will technologies and approaches unique to this project affect the eventual outcome?
10. *Scale:* How will upscaling volume and scope beyond past experience impact project performance?

Even the most perfect construction process can't remove uncertainty from a complex systems development project. Where there is uncertainty, there is risk. Where there is risk, there needs to be a conscious and thoughtful effort to manage it. Instead of asking, "How did they go about building their software?" we can gain a lot more insight into what happened at DIA by asking, "How did they go about managing their risks?"

Risk Management at DIA

In our brief summary of the events at DIA, we asked you to swallow the often-repeated claim that the airport was 100-percent ready to open except for the baggage-handling software, and that the airport couldn't open at all without that software. Let's go over that premise again in some detail.

First of all, maybe the assertion that all the other subprojects were complete wasn't true. Maybe the baggage system was not the only late component, merely the *most visibly* late component. Maybe the whole schedule was hopeless and *everybody* was late. When this happens, a common ploy is for heads of the various subprojects to play a little brinkmanship to assert complete readiness, hoping that one of their peers will crack first. When someone finally cracks, the others just affect to wrinkle their brows in disappointment and then frantically use the extra time to fix up their own domains. Maybe that's what happened at DIA. But just for the purposes of this analysis, let's assume not. Take all the other subproject managers at their word and assume that the airport could indeed have opened but for the failure of the Automated Baggage Handling software. The entire cost of delay—more than $500 million in extra financing—was therefore attributable to the lateness of that one key element.

And now start asking yourself a few key questions:

Q1: Why couldn't the airport open without the baggage-handling software?
That's easy: The baggage-handling software was on the overall project's critical path for the airport's opening. It was so essential to airport operations that the members of the organization's governing board knew they couldn't move passengers through the airport, even for a single day, without that system.

Q2: Why was the ABHS on the critical path?
Well, because there was no other way to move the baggage. The system of tele-carts and bar-code readers and scanning devices and switch points and cart unloaders was the only way to get baggage to and from the planes.

Q3: Are there no alternative ways to move baggage?
Of course. There is, for example, the time-honored method of having big burly guys haul the stuff. There is also the conventional airport approach of small trucks pulling hand-loaded carts, daisy-chained together.

Q4: When the ABHS wasn't ready on time, why couldn't DIA open with one of these alternative methods of moving baggage?
Um. Well. (Hem and haw.) The tunnels that were meant to serve the automated tele-cart system were too low for people and couldn't accommodate the trucks. So the automated system had to work.

Q5: Couldn't the tunnels have been redesigned so that trucks and hauled carts could go through them?
Yes, but there wasn't time. By the time it was discovered that the ABHS software would be late, the tunnels were already built. And the time to revamp them was judged to be longer than the time required to perfect the software.

Q6. Couldn't the revamping of the tunnels have started earlier?
Yes, but that wasn't judged appropriate. Money and time spent on the tunnels would have been wasted had the software actually been delivered on time, as upper management was then assuring it would be.

Q7: Wasn't lateness of the ABHS software seen as a potential risk?
Only after it happened. Before that, the software was placed on an aggressive schedule and managed for success.

Q8: Haven't software projects been late before?
Yes, but this one was supposed to be different.

Q9: Was there any history of prior projects building similar systems?
Yes. The Franz Josef Strauss Airport in Munich had installed a pilot ABHS, designed along the lines of the DIA version.

Q10: Did the DIA team visit the Munich project, and if so, what did it learn?
Members of DIA's ABHS project did visit Munich. The Munich software team had allowed a full two

years for testing and six months of 24-hour operation to tune the system before cut-over. They told the DIA folk to allow that much or more.

Q11: Did DIA management follow this advice?
Since there wasn't time for such extensive testing and tuning, they elected not to.

Q12: Did the project team give sufficient warning of impending lateness?
First of all, the invisible hand of the marketplace made a significant gesture right at the outset. When the DIA board of governors first put the ABHS out to bid, nobody was willing to submit a bid for the scheduled delivery date. All bidders judged that starting the project off with such a schedule was a sure way to court eventual disaster.

Eventually, the airport engaged BAE Automated Systems to take on the project on a best-efforts basis. During the project, the contractor asserted early and often that the delivery date was in jeopardy and that the project was slipping further behind with each month and each newly introduced change. All parties were made aware that they were trying to do a four-year project in two years, and that such efforts don't usually come home on time. All of this evidence was ignored.

Risk Management Practices Honored in the Breach

It's not *how* risk management was practiced at DIA that sunk the project. It's that there was no effort at risk management at all. Even the most perfunctory risk management effort—probably in the first minute of the first risk-discovery brainstorm—would have listed a delay in the software delivery as a significant risk.

An exposure analysis of this risk would have shown that since the baggage-handling software was on the critical path, any delay would postpone the airport's opening, resulting in financial penalties of $33 million per month. (That carrying cost would have been easily calculable from the beginning.) From there, it would have been an obvious conclusion that moving the software off the critical path was a key mitigation strategy. A few million dollars spent early in the effort to make an alternative baggage-handling scheme feasible would have saved half a billion dollars when the software project did not complete on time.

At the very end of this book, we list a dozen or so necessary actions that together constitute risk management. As you will see, DIA upper management methodically observed precisely zero of these.

So, Who Blew It?

Since the contractor has already taken so much heat for its failure to deliver DIA's ABHS on time, it seems only fair to mention here that risk management was not entirely the contractor's job. If you agree with our assessment that this was a failure of risk management far more than of software process, then it makes no sense to blame the contractor. In fact, the risk of the $500 million of extra financing cost belonged at the next level up. Responsibility for risk management accrues to whichever party will have to pay the price for risks that are ignored.

In this case, all such costs were eventually paid for by the contracting agency, Denver Airport System, an arm of the city government. Thus, the city of Denver was responsible for managing the financing risk, something it made no discernible effort to do.

4

THE CASE
FOR RISK MANAGEMENT

"No plan survives contact with the enemy."
—Field Marshal Helmut von Moltke

What our industry can learn from the DIA example is the potential cost of not managing risk. If the previous chapter succeeded, it has left you feeling that you definitely don't want to *not* do this thing called risk management. But still, that may leave you a bit short of actively wanting *to* do it.

What may be required now is a carefully reasoned review of the case for risk management. Presented below is our definitive list of the reasons risk management deserves to be an integral part of your management toolkit.

Risk Management Makes Aggressive Risk-Taking Possible

The reason risk management is hard to do in a typical corporate culture is that it encourages you to deal explicitly with uncertainty. With risk management, you may find yourself telling your client how a risk analysis shows that the window of uncertainty around the delivery date goes all the way from an early, entirely satisfactory date to a range of dates that lie well beyond what he or she may be willing to consider. (In the past, you would probably have just cited the acceptable date and crossed your fingers.)

Of course, there is a chance that the client will walk away when you reveal the extent of the unknown. He or she may be so used to hearing impossible promises—delivery dates guaranteed with great precision at project inception—that your failure to provide one just seems weird.

In the past, you may have resorted to some little white lies to deal with this situation. But people who have been lied to before tend to become cynical. They come to understand that even the most confidently stated outcome is just a shot in the dark. That's the bad rep we software project managers have earned.

To understand how this affects a project's chance of getting started, reverse the situation for a moment. Put yourself in that client's place. Now you're the one seeking someone else to build software for you, software that you urgently need. The project manager who's proposing to do this for you is a likable chap, but he often promises to deliver on a given date and then fails to make it. When he says, "Fine," you hear, "Unlikely." Well, maybe you can live with that. Maybe the uncertainty that you automatically attach to whatever he says is acceptable to you for this project. But suppose not. Suppose the downside of lateness is just too great. What recourse do you have but to choose not to do the risky project? Another opportunity lost.

Project managers often tell us that their clients would never do *any* projects if they understood the downside. Such managers see themselves as doing a positive service to their clients by shielding them from the ugliness that lies ahead. Concealing the potential for delay and failure, as they see it, is a kindness that helps clients marshal sufficient gumption to give the go-ahead. Then, the project can very gently introduce them to bad news, a little bit at a time, as it happens.

The problem is that such clients have memories. They remember other projects that started off with rosy scenarios and soon went sour. The result is that they expect the worst and become risk-averse.

Instead, imagine that a software project manager approaches you and makes a clean breast of his uncertainty about your proposed project: "Look, there are unknowns here, and we have catalogued the following eleven of them." (Here, he shows you his risk list.) "Taken together, these unknowns give us a fairly wide window of uncertainty around the delivery date. Some of the dates within this window will probably be unacceptable to you.

But here is our plan—already decided—for how we will act to contain and minimize the various downside risks, and here is how you will know at any point in the project how we're faring." If, in addition, he could show you past project records that showed how actual results conformed to the uncertainty assessments for those projects, you could begin to believe what you were hearing.

Now at least you know where you stand. You're taking a risk, but you know how much risk. You can say yes. Your willingness to commit to a risky project is a direct function of how well you can logically conclude that the risks have been assessed, quantified, and confronted.

Risk Management Decriminalizes Risk

Can-do thinking pervades our industry. The direct result of can-do is to put a damper on any kind of analysis that suggests *can't-do*. Without the explicit infrastructure of risk management, announcing a risk (particularly one that questions the fondest wishes expressed from on high) can put the announcer in an uncomfortable situation. He or she may be written off as a whiner, as someone with insufficient buy-in, or as a defeatist.

Risk management makes a limited amount of can't-do thinking okay. When you put a structure of risk management in place, you authorize people to think negatively, at least part of the time. Companies that do this understand that negative thinking is the only way to avoid being blindsided by risk as the project proceeds.[1]

Risk Management Sets Up Projects for Success

In the absence of explicitly declared uncertainty, achieving anything but the most optimistic imaginable result is a failure. Without risk management, projects have no way to distinguish between stretch goals and reasonable expectations. The result is that they adopt their stretch goals as schedule and then—since such goals are typically at the hairy edge of possibility—fail to meet them.

Sufficiently jaded stakeholders take steps ahead of time to assure that these failures don't particularly inconvenience them. In fact, what the project perceives as a failure may be a success to the stakeholders (more later about this unfortunate dynamic). To project personnel, though, it still looks like a botch. People have

---

[1]We are indebted to our late colleague Paul Rook for his elegant observation that "risk management decriminalizes risk."

little heart for work that leads them from one failure to another. The cost in morale, burnout, and poor employee retention is substantial.

So often, we see "failed" projects where there is good reason to believe that the managers are able and their people are competent to do the work they've been asked to do. If they weren't, they all would have been shown the door long ago. When one project after another is declared a failure, that just proves that setup conditions for those projects were flawed. Risk management is a way to break this grim cycle by providing a set of meetable goals and schedules and engendering successful projects that look and feel successful from beginning to end.

Risk Management Bounds Uncertainty

If you find yourself marching along a battlefield strewn with corpses, you have a legitimate reason to fear for your own safety. You wonder, What did these poor dead guys learn at the end, that I may be just about to learn myself? Your fear may make you unwilling or even unable to carry on.

If, on the other hand, you have credible evidence that a hundred thousand of your fellow soldiers crossed this field without injury, and the score of bodies you see around you were the only casualties, that changes things substantially. There are still risks, but with such evidence, you can make a thoughtful and informed decision about how to proceed.

Bounded uncertainty may be daunting—it's frightening to come to grips with how little we can be sure of!—but in its absence, we have something worse: boundless uncertainty. Boundless uncertainty makes people either risk-averse or foolhardy. Both are disasters.

Risk Management Provides Minimum-Cost Downside Protection

When you know the uncertainty, you know how much reserve you'll need in order to give yourself sensible protection. The reserve is what you spend on mitigation plus what you hold back to fight fires when they occur.

A risk reserve is, by definition, time and money that you may not need. It takes guts to put a risk reserve into your schedule and budget. But not having one to deploy—as in the case of DIA—means that you will pay far more for the risks that do materialize.

Risk Management Protects Against Invisible Transfers of Responsibility

When there are multiple parties to a development effort (such as client, contractor, and subcontractor), some of the risks will typically accrue to each party. The guiding principle is that responsibility for a risk accrues to whichever party will have to pay for the undesirable outcome caused by that risk. Who pays is a contract matter, but remember that contracting is an imperfect and poorly understood art. Since no party can be confident of having responsibility for zero risks, all need to do some risk management.

In the absence of risk management, subtle transfers of risk responsibility may often go unnoticed. For example, when a client negotiates away a contingency fee that was meant to cover certain risks, responsibility for those risks has likely migrated from the contractor to the client.

Risk Management Can Save Part of a Failed Effort

Projects fail. More importantly, subprojects fail. If you're managing a program of connected efforts, your first concern ought to be that the failure of one component doesn't jeopardize the whole. Again, think of DIA. The overall program could have been buffered—at relatively low cost—from the failure of one element.

Risk Management Maximizes Opportunity for Personal Growth

Since companies that don't manage risk effectively become risk-averse, it follows that they end up taking few risks and no big ones. That means they move into new territory either fitfully or not at all. This is bad for the company (it's becoming a takeover candidate, at best), but it's also bad for employees. No new directions means no personal growth.

Who needs to work for a company that doesn't afford regular opportunities for growth? You won't lose everyone because of this factor—only your best people.

Risk Management Protects Management from Getting Blindsided

Risk management doesn't make problems go away; it merely assures that they won't come at you from out of the blue.

What problems have beset projects that you were on, where you could honestly report that *nobody* could have seen them coming? Damn few, we'll bet. There is almost always some warning before a problem crops up. We have trained ourselves not to look out for these warnings; risk management is trying to undo that training.

Risk Management Focuses Attention Where It Is Needed

Finally, risk management is a focusing mechanism, one that puts your resources where they belong. The opposite of risk management is reckless management. It makes your organization all offense and no defense. Your only winning strategy with that combination is to catch every conceivable lucky break. When luck becomes an integral part of your strategy, you know you're in trouble.

PART II

WHY NOT

- What is the downside of risk management?
- Isn't risk management at odds with the principle of managing for success?
- Is there any reason to believe that risk management will be compatible with our corporate culture?
- What's wrong with counting on a few lucky breaks to make the schedule?
- How do we distinguish between those risks that have to be managed and those that can be safely ignored?

5

THE CASE
AGAINST RISK MANAGEMENT

*"Risk management often gives you more reality than
you want."* —Mike Evans, Senior Vice President
ASC Corporation[1]

We must confess that there are a few reasons *not* to do risk
management. We wouldn't be writing this book if we felt
that such reasons were sufficient to make the whole notion unattractive. Nonetheless, you need to know about the negatives as
well as the positives.

Most of the negatives have to do with the way that risk management interferes with certain management styles. Many of
these styles are generally counterproductive anyway, yet they do
have their followers. Being a good manager is nontrivial. It takes
hard work, gumption, and most of all, talent. People who don't
have the requisite talent fall back on a host of mechanical
approaches, such as Management By Objectives, Parkinsonian
scheduling, and a "culture of fear" to scare their subordinates into
performing. Though these things are not easily defensible, some
managers and some entire organizations are addicted to them.
These practices are incompatible with any risk management
scheme.

---

[1]Mike Evans is a fellow governor of the Airlie Council, a group that was set
up by the U.S. Department of Defense to help the armed services improve software and systems acquisition.

It would be glib of us, though, to suggest that *all* opposition to risk management comes from scared and talent-free managers. There are some very real reasons to be concerned that the approach might not work. The following sections contain our definitive list of the reasons people cite for not doing risk management, and our comments on each one. (The italicized comment under each heading presents our sense of what the spoken objection probably means.)

1. Our stakeholders are not mature enough to face up to risk.

"If we told the truth, our stakeholders would be too scared to do the project, so we have to lie to them."

Lying, in this situation, is a real public service.

In the early days of the software industry, the stakeholders were often clerks and managers of clerical departments. That was because the first functions we tended to automate were clerical. These stakeholders were low-level, relatively powerless, and not very well informed about automation. The typical systems analyst on such a project was usually paid a lot more than most of the stakeholders he or she interacted with.

During this period, IT often affected a paternalistic, "we know best" attitude. Maybe this even worked, on occasion, to help useful systems get built.

Today's stakeholders, however, are different. They are typically more powerful than their IT counterparts, and they have been around for a while. They are savvy about automation. Most of all, they have really good memories.

These days, risk-taking is becoming the norm on more than just IT projects. Your stakeholders are being encouraged to take risks of their own, completely outside the realm of IT. They know about risk. They also know about being lied to. Concealing risk from them is a pretty dumb tactic.

2. The extent of uncertainty is just too much.

"I can cite a window around the date, but not such a big window."

Many software managers are willing in the abstract to confront the uncertainties of their projects, but they are daunted by the size of those uncertainties. If they could use risk management techniques to show a delivery date that's plus or minus 2 percent or 5 percent, they'd be delighted. But the uncertainties in our field are much bigger than that. A careful assessment of potential causes of delay should oblige you to admit something like this: "Delivery can be expected sometime between Month 18 and Month 29, with an 85-percent confidence factor date of Month 24."

The reason you would find yourself believing such a conclusion is that the empirical record of delaying factors and resultant delays has forced you to believe it. But you also know that your organization has been feeding itself on hype for so long that this kind of imprecision will be hard to swallow.

Some organizations are so desperate to believe they're in complete control that if they realize they aren't, they settle for the *illusion* of control instead. The most common symptom of this is a ridiculous precision (a very narrow window of uncertainty) attached to estimates that subsequently turn out to be very inaccurate.

3. Explicit windows of uncertainty excuse poor performance.

> *"If I tell our developers to get the work finished up just any time between July and December, they'll go right to sleep."*

Software managers have tended to follow a standard rule: The estimate and the goal are identical. The discipline of risk management, though, will counsel you to use goals as you always have to help people strive for best performance. At the same time, it will prompt you to use a very different planning estimate when making promises to your clients and management.

4. A "manage for success" approach is better.

> *"Look, we don't do risk management, but we keep an eye on the risks and then we manage to make sure they don't happen."*

You can manage your risks, but you can't make them go away. Any "manage for success" approach based on making sure risks don't materialize just sets a project up for disaster when they do. For any sensibly organized project, the risks are not incidental to the project goal; they come with the terrain. As we discuss in detail later, removal of these intrinsic risks can only be achieved by forgoing much of the value of the product as well.

5. The data needed to do risk management effectively is lacking.

> *"We just don't know enough about the risks that will affect this project."*

Many of the risks facing any given project are, of course, intrinsic to that project. Unique risks arise from the product itself as well as from the cultural and political environment of the project. There won't be much or any data about some of these risks. However, the major risks facing most projects are common to all IT projects. If you only have data on the common ones, you have the wherewithal to contain most of your risk.

6. Risk management in isolation is dangerous.

> *"I dare not be the only one to do risk management honestly."*

While we've tried to pose a reasonable counter to each of the first five reasons (excuses) for not doing risk management, this sixth reason is irrefutable. Risk management makes no sense whatsoever for a single project manager surrounded by peer managers who are practicing pure can-do. By publishing risk lists and quantifying uncertainty, that lone manager will only end up looking like a wimp, or worse, be seen as the carrier of a dangerous infectious disease.

If you work in an organization where risk management is not practiced widely, you may still be able to make use of some of its tools and techniques on your project, but you must not go public with your findings. Telling the truth where optimism (lying) is the norm puts the truth teller at a terrible disadvantage. If you assert that there is only a 10-percent chance of making a hoped-for delivery date, you expose yourself to competition from a hungry peer who may say, "Give me the job, boss, and I'll bring it home for you on time, guaranteed."

The worst organizations penalize unappealing forecasts, but not unappealing results. When the project fails, they reason, "Hey, the guy missed the date, but at least he gave it a good try." This problem feeds upon itself: People understand that promising big is more important than delivering, and everybody learns to act accordingly. If you work for this kind of organization, you might as well go with the flow and keep your risk assessments to yourself.

6

THE ONUS OF UNCERTAINTY

Corporate culture—whatever that means—poses serious challenges to the would-be risk manager. The most important of these is an attitude toward uncertainty that can thwart even the best-intended effort. The attitude is summed up as follows:

> It's okay to be wrong, but not okay to be uncertain.

If that rule describes your company, you're sunk.

The rule says you may miss your promised delivery date—even miss it by a mile—but in the months and days leading up to that date, you're not allowed to express any doubt that you will indeed deliver on time. Failure is tolerated as long as you don't commit the capital crime of admitting beforehand that you *might* fail. Another expression of the rule is that you can ask for *forgiveness* for being late (afterward), but you can't ask for *permission* (beforehand).

If your corporate culture won't allow you to admit uncertainty, you can't do risk management. It's as simple as that. You can learn how it ought to be done, but you can't actually manage your risks. It's as if we had shown you how to play an octave on the keyboard with one hand, but your own hand just isn't large enough to reach.

This constraint may leave you prone to an infectious disorder called *selective myopia*. Projects that are stricken with this condition can only see small problems. Large problems may loom directly ahead—problems that would be in the center of any healthy project's field of vision—but they go completely unseen by the victims of selective myopia.

"Oh, you mean *that* oncoming train"

The symptoms are straightforward. People take elaborate care not to trip over the railroad ties, but nobody can see the oncoming train. Risks are identified, a risk list is published, risks are reported on status reports, and mitigation strategies are approved. Risks are monitored and tracked. If one only reviews the risk lists and records, it appears that the project is low-risk. All the risks enumerated are at the inconvenience or nuisance level. The risk tracking proceeds without variance until the project is suddenly canceled, often followed by a furious bone-picking of the corpse by litigation. Here are a few examples:

- *Patient 1.* A contractor is building a turnkey system for a client. Everything seems to be under control. Issues are out there, but they are noted on the risk list and nothing hints at failure. Then the final system is delivered to the client for acceptance and is rejected outright. The contract called for a mutually approved specification for the new system. No spec was ever accepted. At no time in the project history did anyone add the risk, "We haven't formally agreed on what we're building."

- *Patient 2.* A contractor is building a replacement system for a client that recently merged with another company. The contractor has proposed using a set of software modules from a solutions vendor, along with some customization, as the new system for the merged organization. Packages are purchased, and new hardware is installed. Risks are listed, status meetings are held. From the dawn of the project, the client has repeatedly proclaimed that since the peak of its business is from Labor Day to Christmas, either the new system or some temporary solution must be in place by then. The various client participants on the project repeat this like a mantra. At no time, as the months tick by, does the risk, "We might not have the new system in place by September," appear on any risk list or any project status report. It's just too awful to consider. Labor Day blows by as though it were Arbor Day. There goes Thanksgiving, then Christmas. In January, the CEO of the client company cancels the project, tosses out all contractor personnel, and files a lawsuit.

Variation on the Theme

TDM: *I was working on a litigation effort, looking back over the remains of a project that had gone badly down the tubes. Many things had gone wrong, but the one that actually proved fatal was that a Title-8 subcontractor had been completely overwhelmed by the commitments it had accepted. Eventually, the contractor simply walked. The little company folded and never was heard from again.*

    Interestingly, the project had a risk list. When we went back over the successive versions of the list that had been published from day one right up to cancellation, we found an amazing thing: The risk that the Title-8 subcontractor might fold up its tent had been articulated early in the project, but was then pointedly removed from the list, never to appear again.

This is the same kind of selective myopia we referred to earlier, but practiced after the fact. Management looked aghast at a potentially fatal risk that made it onto the list. As long as it was there, the big boss glared accusingly at everyone. Some poor bastard was instructed to "manage that risk and make damn sure it's sufficiently managed so we can remove it from the list by this time next week."

Fortunately, There's a Vaccine

What is the cause of this can't-see-the-oncoming-train disease? We haven't isolated the virus, but suspicions abound. Maybe these organizations do not have the voluntary muscle structure to utter the word "catastrophe." They persuade themselves they are dealing with all their risks—potential problems—but they are only dealing with a subclass of these: potential problems for which they have remedies.

There may be no cure for those already infected, but there is a vaccine that has shown promising results for keeping the uninfected clean. The vaccine must be administered at the very beginning of any risk management attempt. At the first go-round of what would normally be risk identification, vaccinate everyone by naming all the catastrophic outcomes you can imagine. Ask for more catastrophes from the group. Don't do any risk management—yet. Speak the words "failure," "rejection," and "cancellation." (If you try to say these words and they won't come out, you are already infected and should seek professional help.) If you can say these words, see whether you can get others to speak them publicly as well. Now, work backward from your catastrophe list, asking for scenarios that could lead to each of the catastrophes. Take each scenario in turn and try to describe the risk(s) that could bring it about. Now you have the beginnings of a risk list that might reflect future reality.

We will return to this risk-discovery technique in Chapter 14, laying out its procedures and some tricks for making it work. Just for now, though, the essence of the technique is this: Attack your nightmares, not your petty worries; to discover the risks that really matter to your project, trace backward from effect to cause. Watch for oncoming trains.

7

LUCK

TRL: Good luck on your next project . . . but don't count on it.

When you choose to ignore a risk, you're depending on luck to keep the undesirable thing from happening. This may be a perfectly sensible way to deal with some risks, but not all of them. The "not all" part is essential here because a common pathology is the decision to count on luck to take care of *all* risks.

Just for the record, though, before dealing with the pathology, let's take a look at the kinds of risks that may be sensibly excluded from management.

"We'll take our chances on that one."

Can you think of a real risk (a bad thing that legitimately could happen and which would certainly have awful consequences) that makes no sense to manage? One that's not even worth putting on your list?

The one that often comes up in our risk management seminars is "asteroid demolishes company." What are the characteristics of the asteroid risk that make it not worth managing? We've come up with the following two:

1. The probability of materialization is small enough to ignore.

46

2. Should the risk materialize, it makes the effort under management (the product that you're building) irrelevant.

It may be tempting to add a third characteristic here: There isn't much we can do about the risk should it materialize. While this is true, it is not a legitimate reason alone for choosing to ignore any risk. A given risk may be fatal to a project, but it may not be fatal from the point of view of some participants of that project. Those who are likely to survive must manage the very risk that could prove fatal to the others.

The two numbered reasons listed above give you leave to ignore the asteroid risk. Here are two other valid reasons to excuse yourself from managing risks:

1. The risk has minimal consequences and requires no mitigation.
2. It's somebody else's risk.

Sure, ignore a risk like "Ted may call in sick on Tuesday" because you can safely pay for the loss out of project petty cash (in the time sense). Do be sure, though, that this is *not* one of those risks that only have minimal consequences if you've prepared in advance. If it *is* one of those risks and you want your mitigation effort to be available once your risk moves into transition, you'll need to do your prep work beforehand. (If the risk belongs to someone else, see our discussion in Chapter 9.)

We have identified four good reasons not to manage a given risk. No surprise, most of the risks facing your project will not fall into any of these four categories. The ones that don't are your real and meaningful risks.

Why would you ever find yourself not managing your project's real and meaningful risks, but instead, counting on luck to make them all go away? Well, suppose the project had been conveyed to you in the form of a personal challenge like this one:

"I know April will be tough—that's why I'm giving the job to you!"

When a project comes wrapped as a challenge, it forces you into a posture of counting on a certain amount of luck. If the boss tells you, for example, that you and your eight people are the company's last, best hope to get a key piece of work done by April (*groan,* the CEO's been talking to the press again), what else can you do? What if your boss looks you right in the eye and begs you to *bring this one in for the Gipper?* With that kind of a hand-off, you may be inclined just to do your best and keep your fingers crossed.

You realize that there is no chance of making April without catching some important breaks along the way. Catching those breaks has become an integral part of your project plan. This is the exact opposite of risk management, where your project planning is very much focused on what to do if you don't catch breaks.

Projects that start off as personal challenges seldom have their risks managed sensibly. They depend instead on luck. There's not a lot you can do about it if the project comes to you that way, but you can learn for the future. When you're in a position to engender projects yourself, make sure you don't package them in such a way that luck has to be built into the plan. Offer reasonable stretch goals, but make sure that real expectations make room for the breaks that don't happen.

Shocked, Disappointed, and Dismayed

TRL: *Without knowing anything at all about your current project, I'll bet even money that you'll be late. After all, well over half of all projects deliver late or deliver less than was promised by the original deadline. It's far worse when a project is on an admittedly aggressive schedule. Project people seem disconcerted when I proclaim that I'm willing to bet against them. They try so hard to believe that they'll buck the odds. What usually happens is that everyone agrees that the deadline is very tight; everyone works very hard; and then, when people see that they won't make it, they are shocked, disappointed, and deeply dismayed.*

Somehow, the tactic of professing to be shocked, disappointed, and dismayed when you don't catch all the lucky breaks makes it okay to have followed a plan that depended on catching those breaks. But depending on luck for success is not okay; it's real kid stuff.

The Indy 500 Analogy

Enough about software projects, for the moment. For the next page or so, you're going to be an Indy Racing League driver. There you are behind the wheel of the Panther Racing Penzoil Dallara machine with its huge Aurora engine roaring. This is the maximo racing experience. You downshift going into the third turn and skid slightly, but you come out of it nicely, shifting up and accelerating. Your speed on the straightaway is maybe 220 or 225. You pass one, two cars in a blur, and by golly, you're leading the pack. This is your dream and it's coming true.

Take an instant to get perspective: You've been driving for two hours and fourteen minutes, and it's no wonder you're tired. This is lap 198. There are fewer than five miles between you and the checkered flag. Whatever you do, don't let up. Keep applying the heat, but play it safe because this race is yours to lose. In fact, the only real threat is Team Green. They're still behind you, but not very close. You place yourself tight on the rail and concentrate. Only one little piece of your mind is focused on anything but driving: It's the piece that's listening to the gas alarm. You glance down and see that the needle is on empty. But there are only a few miles left. Your pit crew is waving you in, but a pit stop now means losing. The engine has never sounded better. You bear down, holding your position exactly between Team Green and the finish. The last lap. This is it—you're going to win! But wait, the engine is sputtering. It's coughing; you're starting to lose momentum. Hold on, baby. You urge it on as best you can, but there is no engine now. What the hell, you think, being first across is still a win, even if you're coasting. You coast, nearer and nearer and nearer the line . . . but then you stop, just a few feet short. Team Green goes roaring past.

What just happened? You made a calculated decision to skip the pit stop in order to have any chance at all of winning. You willingly took a chance of not finishing at all in order to hang on to even a remote hope of finishing first.

That makes good sense if you're an Indy 500 racer. But you aren't. (Sorry.) You're a software project manager. The same mind-set on a software project is a disaster. When you take every chance in order to win, you may raise the consequences of losing, far beyond where they need to be.

It's a strange calculus but true: Limiting the extent of your losses in software project work is more important, on average, than doing anything about your wins. Every organization suffers defeats in this business. The ones that get hurt most by their defeats (like DIA) are the losers, no matter that they win a few others.

When you challenge your subordinates to pull out the stops and bring the project home on time (even though the schedule is ludicrous), you need to understand that you're staffing your key positions with NASCAR racers. They will take every chance, ignoring every imaginable downside, in order to preserve—at least for the longest time possible—any thin, little chance of winning.

Call that what you will, but it ain't risk management.

PART III

HOW

- How do we go about risk management?
- Since unknowns are unknown, how can we possibly quantify them?
- What tools are available to help?
- Where does risk management data come from?
- What are risk reserves, and how are they used?
- What can we do about a risk, beyond just tracking it?
- What are the recurrent risks of software projects, and what do we know about them?
- How do we discover risks in the first place?

8

QUANTIFYING UNCERTAINTY

Software development is a risky business because the entire undertaking is shrouded in uncertainty. Anything you need to predict about a project will be to some extent uncertain. But exactly how uncertain?

We can look back at a given project and say about the project manager, "She really didn't know when the work would be done." But what does that mean? *How* uncertain was she? Maybe she was confident that the project would be done sometime in Month 6, and just a little unsure about whether that meant early or late in the month. Or maybe she was truly clueless. There is clearly a world of difference between these two levels of uncertainty. Think about it this way: You are a project manager running an effort that is scheduled to be done by October 30. You've got a pretty good sense that October 30 is not in the cards, but beyond that, you really don't know. You're essentially clueless. Your subordinates are equally in the dark. So, around midsummer, with the deadline four months away, you call in a consultant. The consultant you've chosen is the best in the business, someone who can size up a project in his sleep and tell you where it stands. After a few days of poring over the spec and the interim work products and meeting with your team and stakeholders, he gives you the straight skinny:

> "Listen, there is simply no chance of finishing before the first of next year—zero. The most likely date for

delivery of an acceptable product is the beginning of next April. Even that date is not particularly bankable. You probably don't want to publish any delivery date before May 1. At least with a date in May or later, you'll have a better than fifty-fifty chance of making it. If you want a date you'll have virtually zero chance of missing, you'll have to go all the way out to the end of next December."

You called in a consultant because you were uncertain about when the project would be done, but the consultant has shown himself to be somewhat uncertain as well. The difference between your uncertainty (clueless) and his (described by the preceding paragraph) is that he put definite bounds on his.

Same Idea in Picture Form

Let's take the consultant's assessment and express it as a picture. Since what he was talking about all along was probability ("no *chance* of delivery before the first of next year," "better than fifty-fifty *chance*," and so on), the picture will show certainty/uncertainty as a probability of delivery on any given date. We'll want to extend the picture out to cover the whole range of dates between the virtually impossible to the essentially sure. So, we plot probability on the vertical and time on the horizontal. Here is the empty chart, showing the four explicitly mentioned dates:

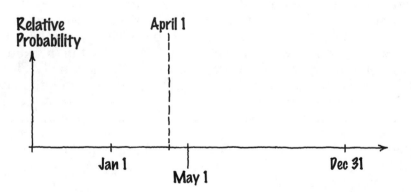

The consultant has told us that the probability of finishing was zero for all days leading up to January 1, that needing more time beyond December 31 of next year was highly unlikely (since he was quite sure the project would be finished by then), and that the most likely date (the day with the highest probability of being the actual delivery date) was April 1. Given this, we can fill in those two ranges and the peak of the curve. Since there is no scale yet affixed to the vertical, we can place the peak arbitrarily, without being concerned yet about its precise value. That gives us the following:

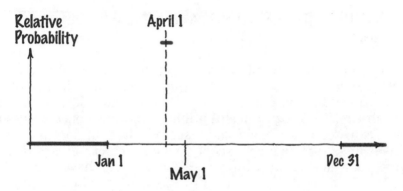

All that's left is to fill in the middle, striving to keep the area under the curve to the left of May 1 more or less equal to the area to the right (more on this later). A smooth curve that fits all these constraints looks like this:

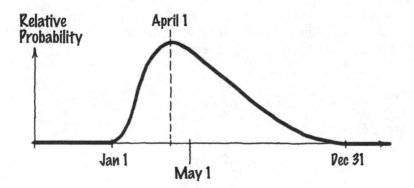

The result is a kind of uncertainty diagram called a *risk diagram*. Risk diagrams are the subject of Chapter 10, so you'll find more there about their characteristics and uses. But for the present, you've probably already figured out most of the essentials:

- The area under the curve represents the cumulative likelihood of finishing by a given date, so if a third of the area lies to the left of April 1, that says that the probability of finishing on or before April 1 is about 33 percent.
- The area under the whole curve is 1.0, representing the consultant's assessment that the work will be completed sometime in the period between January 1 and December 31 of next year.

What the Risk Diagram Tells Us About Today's Common Practices

The risk diagram pictured above might show a lot more uncertainty (a bigger tolerance window around the date) than is typically declared in your organization. If you believe it to represent the truth—reality—then you still might have some concerns about who gets to see it and how it is presented. Even if absolutely no one gets to see the diagram except yourself, the exercise of quantifying your uncertainty with such a diagram can have enormous benefit.

For example, the diagram immediately helps you understand a lot of what's been going on in the software industry over the past few decades. One common plaint that managers share with us is that "the earliest articulated date automatically becomes the deadline." Going public with the consultant's finding that "there is no chance of delivery before the first of next year" may land you in a position where January 1 is therefore laid down in concrete as the deadline. But on the risk diagram, the area under the curve to the left of January 1 is essentially zero:

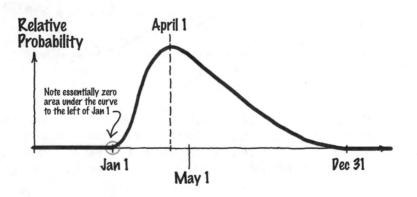

That says that the chance of delivery by the "deadline" is negligible. The pathology of setting a deadline to the earliest articulable date essentially guarantees that the schedule will be missed.

Even the strategy of picking the "most likely date" is not particularly safe, as the area to the left of the peak of the curve is barely a third. That says there is a two-thirds chance of missing the most likely date. Yes, it was most likely of all the dates, but still not *very* likely.

Picking the date that's right in the center—with half the area to the left and half to the right—still only gives you one chance in two of delivering on time. In fact, picking *any* single date off the risk diagram is problematic; what makes a lot of sense instead is to treat the risk diagram itself as the schedule commitment. Admittedly, it has uncertainty in it, but simply picking a date and committing to it does not make that uncertainty go away; it merely conceals your uncertainty from the people who receive your commitment. The test of a grown-up organization is that managers at all levels learn to live with commitments that have explicitly stated uncertainty bounds.

The Nano-Percent Date

The intersection of the curve with the horizontal defines the first date that has a nonzero probability. But it's not very nonzero. This intersection is what we call N, the "nano-percent date," since delivery by that date is about a nano-percent likely.

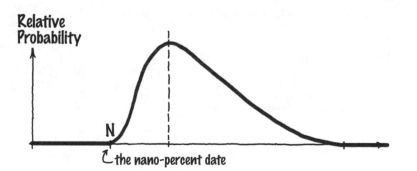

the nano-percent date

It makes no sense at all to commit to a delivery at N, but it is an important date nonetheless. It's important because it is something that we have an innate sense for. All of our estimating experience so far has taught us how to estimate N, but then it erroneously guided us to treat N as a delivery date. This second step is poor practice, but our hard-learned experience in figuring out the nano-percent date can and will be turned to our advantage.

Yes, a Window, but How Much of a Window?

In mature organizations, uncertainty diagrams are everywhere. They show explicitly what's known and what isn't. If everybody is definitely hoping to have a new product out the door by a given date, the uncertainty diagram keeps everybody focused on just how likely or unlikely that date is.

Explicitly stated uncertainty allows you to take risks. Without it, you can still take on minor risks, but serious, competent managers are never going to take on any big risk without credible assurance of just how big a risk it is. Concealing the extent of the uncertainty doesn't help gull these managers into taking risks that they probably ought to take. Instead, it breaks down the managers' trust in the very people they need to depend upon when the risks are high.

Now, all of that would be easy enough to swallow if the window of uncertainty could be kept small. But can it? You can certainly imagine being the world's greatest advocate of risk diagrams if the one for your project looked like this:

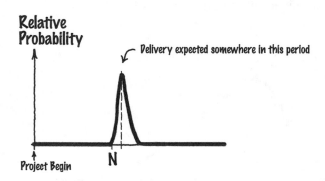

Here, the window of uncertainty seems like a reasonable proportion of the optimal duration from project inception to N.

But suppose instead that your risk diagram looked like this:

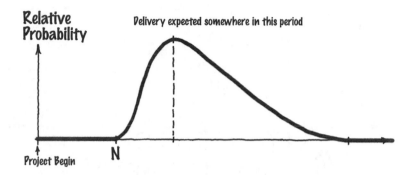

What's so unappetizing about this picture is that uncertainty is large compared to the interval from Project Begin to N.

If you're like the rest of us software project managers, you feel comfortable when the total window is on the order of 10 to 15 percent of the time to N, and uncomfortable with anything larger than that—in fact, you're increasingly uncomfortable as the window grows beyond 15 percent.

The rough and tumble of past projects and their politics has acculturated us to think that uncertainty windows of 10 to 15 percent of N are proper. Larger windows seem wrong, somehow undisciplined. Many managers even consider them wimpy.

However, none of this matters at all. The size of your window of uncertainty is a function of how much noise (variation) there is in your organization's development processes, and it has nothing to do with anybody's sense of what is proper.

Process noise is the source of deviation from one project to the next, the explanation of why some projects take longer compared to your best efforts. More or less, process noise is a quantification of the effects of past risks. The amount of noise can be empirically determined for any organization that keeps even rudimentary records of its performance. This figure establishes how much uncertainty there must be about your next projection. In other words, your past performance determines window size.

For the software industry as a whole, window size is in the range of 150 to 200 percent of N. So, for a project with N at Month 25, the tail end of the uncertainty curve will go as far out as Month 75. You're not required to feel particularly happy about this. It's just the way things are. Pretending otherwise won't help.

9

MECHANICS OF
RISK MANAGEMENT

*"We aren't really bad at estimating. What we are
really bad at is enumerating all the assumptions that
lie behind our estimates."*

—Paul Rook[1]

An easy test of risk awareness in a project is this: Look
through the project plan and ask the manager to indicate any
tasks that might not have to be done at all. You may suddenly
find yourself on the receiving end of a baffled expression. Put
into words, that confused look seems to ask, *If a task doesn't have
to be done, why on earth would we ever put it into the plan?*
You've just learned that the plan, in this manager's view, is the set
of all tasks that definitely have to be done.

Maybe We're Not So Bad at Estimating

When a project strays from schedule, it's seldom because the
work planned just took longer than anyone had thought; a much
more common explanation is that the project got bogged down
doing work that wasn't planned at all. Our work as litigation consultants provides new examples of this every year. The bulk of
this evidence has led us to the following, initially startling, conclusion:

---

[1]Paul Rook, from his keynote on risk management, European Conference on
Software Methods, London, October 1994.

> Most software project managers do a reasonable job of predicting the tasks that *have to be done* and a poor job of predicting the tasks that *might have to be done.*

There is bad news and good news here. The bad news is that since all real-world projects produce their share of surprises, managers often fail to deliver on their promises, sunk by those "might have to be done" tasks that subsequently need doing. The good news is that these conditional tasks are, at least at a coarse level, fairly predictable.

Yesterday's Problem

A simple list of an organization's top twenty-or-so problems encountered on projects over the past few years is a pretty good initial risk list for its next project. This suggests a totally mechanical beginning to the business of risk management: Run a few postmortems of projects good and bad and look for ways in which they deviated from their initial expectations. Trace each deviation back to its cause and call that cause a risk. Give it a number and carry on.

The principle underlying this approach is this:

> Yesterday's problem is today's risk.

There is a part of each of us that has trouble with this formulation. We want to "correct" it to something like *Today's problem is yesterday's risk,* or *Today's risk is tomorrow's problem.* Such restatements have a surface likeability, but they don't do much for you. It's the equation of past problem with present risk (in other words, a recognition of the repeating nature of project problems) that gives you a leg up on how to practice risk management. If you find that a project you just completed ran into trouble when a few key employees left the company, then personnel loss is *automatically* entered onto your new project risk list. The word "automatically" is worth stressing here: Loss of people, particularly key people, is such a defeat that can-do management may refuse to consider it. Never underestimate the seductive comfort of "Erghhhh, I just don't want to think about that."

So, one way to populate your risk list—at least initially—is through the methodical use of postmortem results. This assumes that your company is already enlightened enough to perform a postmortem analysis at the end of each successful or unsuccessful project, to understand what happened. If you're not doing that, you might want to take a look at the References for two recommendations on postmortem analysis.

Project postmortems are hardly new. What is new is use of the output of the postmortem process as input to the risk management process:

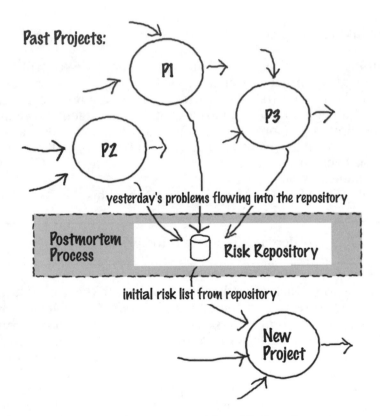

Project problems tend to repeat with sufficient frequency so that if you've analyzed half-a-dozen past projects, you probably have enough data. Keep in mind that postmortem data is only one source of risk information. There is also the risk-discovery process, which we treat in a later chapter.

Okay, We Listed the Risks—Now What Do We *Do* About Them?

The minute you add a risk to your list, there will be pressure to take it off. A risk is an annoyance, and as the annoyance persists from one status meeting to the next, you're liable to see some upper manager showing signs of exasperation. He or she would obviously feel a lot better if you could simply strike the stupid thing off your list and say, "No need to worry about that one, boss; it's taken care of." The more worrisome the risk is, the greater the pressure to make it go away. In our experience, sufficiently exasperated upper managers have a reduced need to understand just why the risk has gone away, as long as it's gone.

Fortunately, some risks *expire* during the course of a project. Perhaps you were worried that one of your subcontractors would fail to deliver a needed component; the risk of non-delivery expires when the subcontractor delivers and the component passes acceptance testing. By the end of the project, all the risks that didn't materialize have expired.

Managers who are applying pressure to do something about risks (in other words, to make them go away) are not likely to be content waiting for them to expire. They want something done *now.* So, what somethings might you be able to do? We identify four things you can do about a risk:

- You can *avoid* it.
- You can *contain* it.
- You can *mitigate* it.
- You can *evade* it.

You *avoid* a risk when you don't do the project or the part of the project that entails the risk. The natural consequence of avoiding a risk is that you forgo the benefit that going into the risky area offered. For example, Merrill Lynch *avoided* the risks of moving into Web trading during the early 1990's. In doing so, the company had to forgo the benefits of increased product distinction and improved branding.

You *contain* a risk when you set aside sufficient time and money to pay for it, should it materialize. In practice, it doesn't make much sense to contain a single risk; instead, you contain your entire set of risks. Some of them will materialize and others won't. A containment strategy sets aside enough resources, on average, to offset the risks that are likely to materialize. We'll offer more about how to do this in a later section.

You *mitigate* a risk when you take steps before its material-ization to reduce eventual containment costs. These are the steps required in advance so that the containment strategy you've chosen will be implementable at transition time.

You *evade* a risk when you do none of the above and the risk just happens not to come back and bite you. It doesn't mate-rialize. When you plan to evade a risk, it is customary to cross your fingers.

The first three of these cost money: Avoidance costs you lost benefit; containment costs you the portion of risk reserves that gets used up; mitigation costs you whatever you spend to reduce containment cost. Only risk evasion appears to be free.

When you are fortunate enough to dodge the bullet, it in fact costs you nothing. For example, you worried that key people would leave during the project, but they didn't; you worried that your supplier would be late, but he wasn't; you worried that the users would balk at your rudimentary interface, but they swal-lowed hard and said okay. You worried about these things, but you didn't do anything about them. In spite of the happy out-come, you didn't really do any risk management, because of this key point:

> Risk management is not the same as worrying about your project.

As it turns out, you *evaded* all three risks. Like the shipowner in Clifford's example, you have not been proved right. You have only been "not found out" to be wrong. There is a difference.

We all evade some risks sometimes and are happy for it. *Planning* on evading risks, however, is hardly a good strategy. Even a short risk list with only a dozen items on it suggests a very low probability of evading all twelve. If each one is only 10-percent likely, the chance that at least one of the twelve will come back to bite you is nearly 75 percent.[1]

This is worth talking about because some companies have the rather pathological characteristic of making risk evasion a per-formance objective. In such a company, risk management is futile; the entire risk management effort looks like nothing more than another cost to be reduced.

---

[1]That is, one minus the twelfth power of 0.9.

Somebody Else's Risk

TRL: *A customer of mine, enticed by the siren song of a vendor's presentation slides, agreed to purchase the latest version of a software package. Strictly speaking, this version was not exactly in the marketplace yet, but the customer received assurances that it was "in the bag." The customer agreed to hire a Vendor Authorized Contractor to manage the project and to get the new application installed within a few months, by the end of that May.*

The Vendor Authorized Contractor did some risk management. Its manager supplied a risk list of twelve items. All of them were concerned with ways that the customer might not live up to the bargain (the customer might delay the project by making decisions very slowly, the customer might not supply adequate workspace to the Vendor Authorized Contractor, and so on).

By now, you should be ready for the next development: The risk that actually sank the project (the vendor's software wasn't delivered in time to make the May operational date) was not even mentioned in the risk list. No one even named the risk until so late in the game that it was no longer a risk, but a problem. To make matters worse, the software was on the critical path.

The first runnable version of the software finally appeared well after the project had been canceled and the lawyers had been called in.

This story brings into focus the complicated problem of risk management in a contracted development project. The key danger in such a situation is a misunderstanding about who manages which risks. The client has every right to nominate certain risks for the contractor to manage, and vice versa. If you are the client, your safest posture is to assume that only those risks specifically allocated to the contractor are his, and that all the rest are yours. Incentives or penalties in the contract allocate risk.

The contractor's risks are those that endanger the successful completion of the contract or diminish the value of completion to the contractor. Everything else is judged by the contractor to be somebody else's risk, and thus a candidate for exclusion from his risk management. That means that you, as the client, have to manage these risks or no one will.

A common class of litigation arises out of projects in which the client is surprised to find that certain important risks never made it onto the contractor's radar. Usually, fault lies with a contract that failed to assign those risks. As a general rule, there are no contracts that successfully transfer *all* responsibility to a single party. If you are either client or contractor, expect to have to do some risk management.

Risk Exposure

Risk exposure is the *expectation* of containment cost. Expectation, as we've used the term here, is a synthetic concept borrowed from probability theory. It is some combination of the probability that the risk will materialize and the cost you will incur if it does. In the simplest case,

$$\text{risk exposure} = \text{cost} \times \text{probability}$$

So, if you identify a risk that is 20-percent likely to occur, and it will cost you a million dollars if it does, your risk exposure is $200,000.

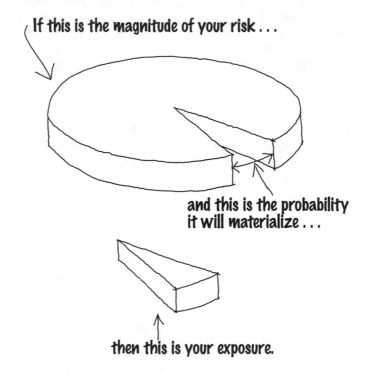

If this is the magnitude of your risk . . .

and this is the probability it will materialize . . .

then this is your exposure.

You can be perfectly sure that the actual cost to pay for a given risk will never be exactly equal to the exposure. The risk cited above, for example, will either materialize or not. If it does, it will cost you a million dollars; if it doesn't, it will cost you nothing. Nonetheless, the exposure associated with that risk is $200,000.

If you calculate exposure for all your risks and set aside a risk reserve equal to the total exposure, that risk reserve will, on average, be sufficient to pay for the risks that do materialize. You may end up short on some projects and have some reserve left on others, but over the long run, your risk reserve will be about right.

Assessing exposure is not a well-defined science. Your best guess about likely materialization may come from industry data, previous problem lists, the risk repository, or just a flat-out guess. Don't excuse yourself from this essential act just because any answer you come up with will never be demonstrably correct. Whether the likelihood of an oncoming train plowing into your project is 25 percent as opposed to 35 percent is not nearly as important as the understanding that there may be a train coming. Get the risk onto your census and start scanning the horizon for plumes of smoke from the locomotive.

So far, we've treated containment as a money matter. You will probably also need to contain risks in a time sense. Risk exposure can be expressed in months of expected delay. If a risk is 20-percent likely to occur and will cost you five months if it does, your time-denominated risk exposure is one month of delay.

A Word About Showstoppers

When evaluating risks for cost and probability, you will probably come across a few that are difficult to price because they cost . . . everything! These risks are your showstoppers; should they materialize, they will stop you dead in your tracks. They will force you either to completely rethink the product or to fold up your tents and cancel the entire project.

Identification of one or more showstoppers does not invalidate the risk management process, even though they resist proper quantification. They represent an inherently different kind of risk, one that calls for an entirely different treatment. Showstoppers can only be managed by what we call *project assumptions*. In order for you to continue your work, you must assume that the showstoppers will not occur. Should any one of these assumptions prove false, you will have to escalate the issue to those above you. Showstoppers are beyond the responsibility and authority of the project.

Here are a few showstoppers we've come across:

- A company embarks on a project to completely reinvent a backbone product. Project management expects this effort to take somewhere on the order of two to two-and-one-half years. There is a chance that one of the competitors will deliver the same product well before the anticipated project complete date.
- A new product is being built to run on the dominant OS used within a target market. What if that OS is upgraded to an incompatible version?

You might be inclined to be fatalistic about such a risk, to say that if it hits you, you're dead, so there's no sense in even looking out for it. You can't control it, so relax and just deal with what you can reasonably expect to handle. There is something very wrong about this logic. For example, imagine yourself promoted two levels in your organization. Now tell us, Aren't you suddenly very, very interested in this risk? You have just discovered that it's not the project team itself but the people who gave birth to your project who own these risks. Those who give can take away. They will have to decide what to do if any of the project assumptions turn false.

The rule here is that a risk owned above you in the hierarchy is an assumption to you. The risk still belongs on your risk list (since you still need to watch it), but it should be explicitly noted as a project assumption. That means it's not going to be managed by you and must therefore be managed by your boss or your boss's boss. You would do well to make a little ritual of passing this risk upward. When you present your risk management plan, formally delegate the management of some risks upward, to someone above you in the hierarchy. You can only do this in the context of a respectable effort on your part to manage the rest of the risks.

Risk Reserve

A risk reserve is a buffer of time and money set aside to contain risks. As we mentioned earlier, one sensible containment strategy is to allocate a reserve that's equal to your exposure. If you follow this strategy, you will be as likely to end up with *unused* reserve as to need some *extra*—as likely to finish *before* your buffered delivery date as *after*.

A more defensive strategy would be to allocate something more than aggregate exposure, while a less defensive strategy would be to allocate less. If you allocate 0 percent of your calculated exposure, you're back where you started.

In the following graphic, the gray area is your most optimistic manpower-loading plan over time, expressed in dollars. The white area is the budget reserve that you will need to allocate in order to compensate for a probabilistic expectation of materialized risks.

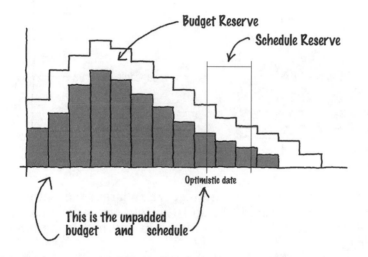

The optimistic project plan (in gray) shows an earlier delivery date than that of the buffered (gray plus white) project plan. The difference between the two dates is your schedule reserve. By setting budget and schedule reserve equal to budget and schedule exposure, you are allocating a reserve that is sufficient, on average, to contain your risks.

Mitigation Costs

Mitigation also costs money. Mitigation activities add to the shaded area of the project plan since they pay for tasks that are 100-percent likely to happen. Mitigation is by definition something that occurs before materialization, so its cost cannot be saved if the risk happens not to materialize. Added mitigation cost is more than offset by reduced containment cost; otherwise, it wouldn't be worth the expense.

In the following two graphics, we show how the upper managers of DIA could have assessed the value of building dual-use tunnels to mitigate the risk of late ABHS software. The first figure shows the project plan with no mitigation:

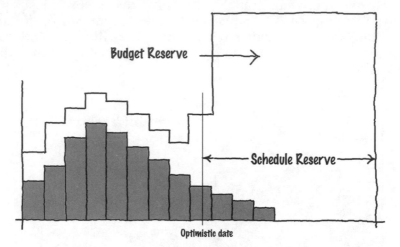

Without mitigation, the schedule reserve is large; the entire airport project will be stalled if the software project is delayed. The budget reserve then has to be enormous to pay for the additional cost of financing.

Contrast this situation with the mitigating action of building dual-use tunnels, early in the project:

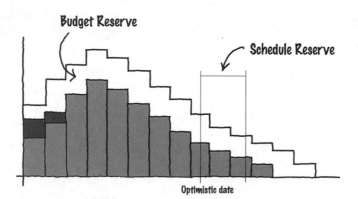

Both reserves are now considerably reduced, but *the shaded area is larger.* It has been increased by the darker portions shown in the first two columns. This is the cost of mitigation, the added cost of the larger tunnels. The schedule has also been stretched out somewhat to the right, about one column width, since mitigation has a time cost as well as a dollar cost. The result is that the optimistic date on the graph is somewhat less optimistic than it was in the no-mitigation plan.

The mitigation plan's rosy scenario (the best case, possible only when all risks fail to materialize) is less rosy than the rosy scenario of the no-mitigation plan. How can that be good? Here's how:

- The area under the outer curve (representing realistic cost) is less than in the no-mitigation case.
- The total of the optimistic date plus the schedule reserve (representing the realistic delivery date) is shorter than in the no-mitigation case.

Transition Indicators and Transition Monitoring

For each managed risk, you need to choose one or more early indications of materialization. Then, watch them like a hawk so you can activate your contingency plan in a timely manner, if necessary.

It's tempting to say that the earliest possible indicator is the only one worth watching, but the problem is a bit more complicated than that. The earliest indicator may expose you to false-positive signals. You'd be ill-advised, for example, to make travel plans based on a five-day weather forecast if waiting for the 24-hour forecast (which is bound to be more accurate) would still leave you sufficient time to act.

On the other hand, the indicators that are least likely to yield false positives may appear too late to be useful. As an example of this, consider the trucker's maxim:

> Every rolling ball precedes a running child.

While it's not strictly true that *each and every* rolling ball is an indicator that a kid is about to come hurtling out under your wheels, you would still be well-advised to hit the brake as soon as you see the ball.

Your choice of transition indicator requires a thoughtful assessment of urgency and of the cost of false-positive triggering.

10

RISK MANAGEMENT
PRESCRIPTION

Most of what still remains to be described is detail. The preceding chapters have put enough of the basic concepts on the table so that we can now lay out a general prescription for what it means to do risk management.

What It Means to Do Risk Management

Risk management is essentially the performance—integrated into the project—of the following nine steps:

1. Use a risk-discovery process (details in Chapter 14) to compile a census of the risks facing your project.
2. Make sure all of the core risks of software projects (details in Chapter 13) are represented in your census.
3. Do all of the following homework on a per-risk basis:

   - Give the risk a name and unique number.
   - Brainstorm to find a transition indicator—the earliest practical indication of materialization—for the risk.
   - Estimate the cost and schedule impact of risk materialization.
   - Estimate the probability of risk materialization.
   - Calculate the schedule and budget exposure for the risk.

- Determine in advance what contingency actions the project will need to take if and when transition occurs.
- Determine what mitigation actions need to be taken in advance of the transition to make the selected contingency actions feasible.
- Add mitigation actions to the overall project plan.
- Write all the details down on a template like the one in Appendix B.

4. Designate showstoppers as project assumptions. Perform the ritual of passing each of these risks upward.
5. Make a first pass at schedule estimation by assuming that *no risks will materialize.* In other words, your initial estimating step is to determine the nano-percent date, the earliest date by which you can't yet prove to yourself that you won't be done.
6. Use local and industry-wide uncertainty factors (details in Chapter 13) to construct a risk diagram with intersection at N.
7. Express all commitments using risk diagrams, explicitly showing the uncertainty associated with each projected date and budget.
8. Monitor all risks for materialization or expiration, and execute contingency plans whenever materializations occur.
9. Keep the risk-discovery process going throughout the project, to cope with late-apparent risks.

These steps are easy enough to list, but a bit more difficult to do. A few comments are in order:

N-Based Scheduling

The premise underlying our N-based scheduling approach is that your natural inclination toward optimism and your experience to date (together with whatever tools you may have available to help you) make you reasonably adept at figuring out N, the most optimistic possible schedule for the project. The difference between ours and the conventional approach is that we propose that you not make a commitment to deliver at N, but that you use N as input to the process of determining a more sensible commitment, one that you can accept subject to the limited uncertainty shown by your risk diagrams.

Of course, N-based scheduling can be abused. Someone who is desperate to get you to commit to a 12-month delivery, for example, may try to assert that N is four months, and that therefore your risk diagram should be based at 4. But the burden of proof is on the asserter here: He or she has to show that four months is at least technically feasible and consistent with optimal performance in the same context on past projects.

Commitments and Goals

Imagine that the risk diagram for your project shows N in March and a 75-percent confidence level for September delivery. Based on this, you may elect to commit to your stakeholders to have a product in their hands by September. September is a sensible commit date, but a less-than-ideal goal for you to convey to your project members. Nobody wants to work toward a goal that is 75-percent sure, that is so little a stretch goal. Similarly, N is not a good goal for the project, since nobody wants to work toward a goal that is 0-percent likely—we've all spent far too much of our lives in that fruitless pursuit. What does make excellent sense is to set a stretch goal for the project somewhere between N and the commit date.

This is new and different: a project with a scheduled commit date that is different from the stretch goal. The rule in most companies has long been

Schedule = Goal = N ✒ *really dumb equation*

N is a mean-spirited goal because it's unreachable. And it's a disastrous commit date for the same reason. What we're proposing instead is

Schedule > Goal > N ✒ *more sensible*

If we've persuaded you that this makes good sense, don't automatically assume that everybody in your organization will see it that way. The bad habit of committing to deliver at N is deeply ingrained. We need to break ourselves of it, but you have to expect—as in breaking any other bad habit—a certain amount of pain along the way.

TRL: *My father is a mathematician, a retired professor of math. He chided me one day about all the software projects that seem to come in late, more or less 100 percent of them.*

"Why is that?" he asked.

I told him, "Well, there are just two possible outcomes for a project: It can be done on time, or it can be done late. I guess the odds seem to favor late, except in a few very remarkable cases."

"There aren't just two possible outcomes, Tim," he responded. "There is a third: Early."

That got me thinking. I visit companies all the time where early is utterly inconceivable. A manager who finished early would be accused of unconscionable gaming of the schedule and would probably be drummed out of the corps.

By making the third result, early, effectively illegal, we have reduced the odds of on-time delivery to nearly zero. Our anti-gaming measure has made gaming the schedule the rule rather than the exception.

We need to make early delivery legal again in order to inspire confidence in our commit dates. This, too, is going to require some serious work on corporate culture. As soon as we make it safe for a project to come home *ahead* of schedule, our stakeholders can begin to have some reasonable expectation of delivery *on* schedule. We can realistically assign goals that are different from commit dates, and we can begin the long-post-poned business of demonstrating to all that we can meet the commitments we make.

Uncertainty Trade-Offs

You can certainly imagine a project for which the delivery date has to be fixed in advance and offers no option of lateness. Showing your boss a risk diagram with poor certainty of making that date will not serve you well.

Fortunately, you have some options for trading off schedule uncertainty for functional uncertainty. If the date is utterly fixed, then you need to express the uncertainty of your project with a risk diagram like this:

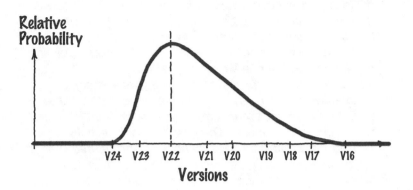

The date is now fixed and the uncertainty is entirely a matter of what will be delivered on that date. If absolutely no risk materializes, all of the functionality of Versions 1 through 24 (represented by V24) can be delivered. Since the odds of evading each and every risk are extremely low, this is the nano-percent functionality—it's not impossible, only extremely unlikely. Judging from the area under the curve to the left of V21, the functionality of Versions 1 through 21 appears to be approximately 50-percent likely by the date. If the stakeholders are adamant that nothing less than V22 will be useful to them, the diagram shows that you have barely a 30-percent probability of giving them what they need. Again, this may be unwelcome news, but concealing it only delays (and worsens) the eventual day of reckoning.

Three caveats here: First, this approach only makes sense if you commit in advance to a highly incremental implementation, and if you lock in, in advance, what the functional extent will be of each version. If you're planning on delivering in only two or three versions, the resultant uncertainty diagram is practically meaningless. And if you defer the decision on what functions are included in which version, your users will be unable to assess what functionality is at risk.

Second, beware of the project that is presented with a fixed deadline but doesn't really have one:

TDM: I was consulting on a project in upstate New York that had a "firm, fixed deadline." The product absolutely had to be delivered by end of the second quarter, no excuses. But it wasn't. In fact, it was finally delivered more than eighteen months late. In retrospect, I *couldn't help wonder what all the song and dance about "firm, fixed deadline" was really about, since the deadline was clearly neither firm nor fixed.*

This was a rare case when I had such an easy relationship with the stakeholder that I could simply ask that uncomfortable question and get a pretty straightforward answer. So I did. He told me—over beers—that what he'd been most concerned about was that the cost would get out of hand. The deadline he'd initially set had no particular time significance, but he figured that the project could only use up a limited amount of money in that time. When the time was up, he could see that he was getting his money's worth from the development team, so he bought into the revised schedule.

Some fixed deadline projects really do have to be done on time (say your company wins the contract for CNN's election night forecasting software). Other fixed deadline projects, like the one described above, have an arbitrary deadline that has nothing to do with a real need on that date. In either case, you'll want to respond with a highly incremental implementation. That much incrementalism has a cost, though; in the second case, much of that cost is wasted.

Incrementalism also doesn't do much for you if there is a significant likelihood that not even the first version can be delivered by the fixed date:

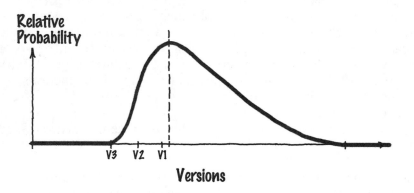

Here we see a project that has a probability of 60 percent or more of arriving at the guaranteed date with not even its first version working.

A Note on Publication of the Risk Census

This may seem like a minor point, but if the politics of your situation allow it, you definitely want to make your risk census public. Keeping the census close to your chest deprives the other stakeholders of a way to monitor the project to see which breaks they're catching and which ones they're not. Distribute the risk list and its associated actions to every single stakeholder, if you can, so that nobody can ever act surprised. Public risk management keeps all eyes on the very factors that will matter most to project success. Finally, a public census of risks enables all personnel to take part in the ongoing risk-discovery process.

As we hinted in Chapter 5, you can only feel safe publishing your risk census if your peer managers are publishing theirs as well. (Being the only honest person in a room full of liars puts you at a dreadful disadvantage.) The organization is far better off when all risk lists are public, since the omission by any manager of a core risk stands out glaringly. Managers who overcommit by ignoring important risks are exposed by a simple comparison of the lists. Instead of looking good for committing ambitiously, they look a little foolish for not acknowledging their risks.

11

BACK TO BASICS

In this chapter, we go back over the basics of risk, risk diagrams, and the interaction of risk management with the more familiar roles of project management. Our purpose in this second pass is to add a bit of rigor to the fast-and-loose presentation of the introductory chapters.

The Hidden Meaning Behind "I Don't Know"

An essential part of project management is coming up with answers to key questions such as, When will you be done? What mean-time-to-failure will your product exhibit? Will your user accept and use the product? All of these are money questions since they deal directly with the cost/value trade-off of the product to be delivered.

One honest answer to all of these questions is, "I don't know." Of course you don't know. The person who is asking you *knows* that you don't know. Questions about future outcomes and the very concept of knowing are mutually incompatible.

One approach is to preface whatever answer you come up with by saying, "I don't know, but . . ." However, even if you don't begin with this qualifier, it is implicitly understood.

Our point here is that you need to recognize these I-don't-know questions because they are always indicators of risk. Whatever you don't know has a downside that can turn against you, and that is your risk. If you could compile all the unique I-don't-know questions about your project and get to the root cause of each one's unknown, you'd have a complete list of the project's risks.

A tactic that is intrinsic to risk management is to listen to yourself saying "I don't know" (out loud or mentally) and force yourself each time to ask the subsidiary question:

> What do I know (or what *could* I know) about what I don't know?

There is always some information available about the unknown. And you are always better off having that information than proceeding without it.

Here's an example. You plant your garden on March 31, and since there is no water handy at the garden site, you're counting on rain to water it for you. So, the money question here is, How much rain will fall on the garden? Your answer, of course, is, *I don't know.* Clearly, this signals a risk that your effort and the cost of your seed may be lost due to insufficient moisture for proper germination. You now ask the subsidiary question: What do I know (or what could I know) about what I don't know? A quick Web search or a visit to your county's agricultural agent is likely to produce the following kind of information about past rainfall in your area:

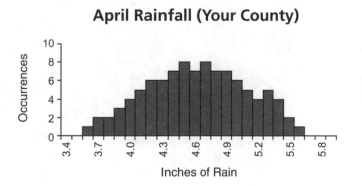

April Rainfall (Your County)

What's shown here is a historical record of the past hundred years of April rainfall in your county. If the information from your seed supplier suggests that germination requires only two inches of watering during the first month, you can feel pretty confident that the extent of your risk is small. Suppose you need at least 4.4 inches? Well, now the risk is more serious. You can see from the chart that in nearly a third of the past hundred years, April rainfall has been less than that amount.

You still don't know what the rainfall will be this year. But what you now know about your unknown is of value. It guides you in planning how to cope with your uncertainty. If a given mitigation scheme (such as arranging to have a pipe installed all the way back to the house) is expensive, you have some useful input to your decision on whether or not to mitigate.

Uncertainty Diagrams (Risk Diagrams) Again

No surprise here, the rainfall chart you've been looking at is an uncertainty diagram. Our formal definition is this:

> **uncertainty diagram** *n: a graphic that shows a set of enumerated outcomes along the horizontal, with the vertical scale showing the relative likelihood of each outcome*

When the thing you're uncertain about has financial significance to your project, its diagram is called a risk diagram.

An uncertainty diagram shows a pattern of past outcomes:

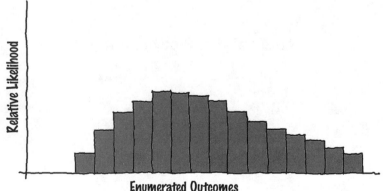

By convention, we scale the vertical so that the sum of all the likelihoods is equal to one.

For most I-don't-know questions, reviewing the pattern of the past is essentially the best you can do to understand the extent of your uncertainty about the future. It doesn't answer your question, but it does give you a handle on the extent to which you don't know the answer. It helps you to locate yourself along the uncertainty scale from Clueless to Confident.

A Better Definition of Risk

Let's shift from the garden example to a more immediately worrisome one, the uncertainty about when your software project will be done:

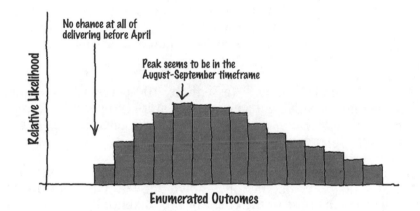

Spot us for the moment that you're ever going to be able to come up with such a diagram for your project, and let's focus first on what good it will do for you if you can.

You can use a risk diagram to quantify the extent of any given risk. For example, you can look for the point at which half the area is to the left and half is to the right and call that your fifty-fifty risk, the earliest outcome for which the likelihood of exceeding catches up with the likelihood of not exceeding. You can look farther out to the right where 90 percent of the area is included (looks like approximately May of next year) and know that if you assert that as your delivery date, you have only a 10-percent likelihood of needing more time. In other words, it's far more likely that you'll come in early than late. You could also exclude the most optimistic 10 percent and the most pessimistic 10 percent and assert that you have an 80-percent chance of finishing sometime between this May and the next. A risk diagram is a tool for assessing the extent of risk, in whatever form you choose to express it. However, we're going to urge a more grandiose under-standing of the risk diagram upon you, the idea that the situation portrayed by the diagram *is* the risk. This leads us to the following final definition of risk, replacing the temporary definition given in Chapter 2:

> **risk** n: *a weighted pattern of possible outcomes and their associated consequences*

In defining risk this way, we're trying to wean you off the habit of thinking numerically about risk and to encourage you instead to think about it graphically. In the past, a question from your boss like, "What is the risk that we won't be ready by the first of next year?" has always seemed to beg for a percentage answer, either explicit or inferred:

- "It's in the bag, boss" (essentially 100-percent certain); or,
- "I guess we've got an even shot at it" (50 percent); or,
- "We really don't have a snowball's chance in hell" (less than a percent).

With our now-refined concept of risk, we answer the question with a risk diagram, like the one shown above. We don't digest the answer for the boss or the client or the stakeholder, but instead lay all the cards on the table: "As you always understood, there is uncertainty in the process of making software, and here is the extent of it for this project."

Characteristics of Risk Diagrams

Some of the uncertainty diagrams we've shown you were simple bar charts where the bars corresponded exactly to the enumerated outcomes. And others were smooth curves. What's the differ-ence? Take the diagrams below, for example: How is the rainfall diagram on the left different from the one on the right?

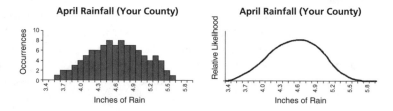

The difference is entirely a matter of granularity. With data from only a hundred years, the curve of the left graph is bumpy and the bars need to be wide enough to be visible. If we had data from a million years, the curve would smooth out substantially and the bars could be made ever thinner, thus producing the more continuous curve shown on the right.

For practical purposes, local data (the results of the handful of projects that you've observed in your company) tends to be of coarse granularity, and industry trends, including thousands of projects, tend to be smooth. Without too much loss of rigor, we can always approximate a granular curve with its smooth near-equivalent.

Risk diagrams often have fairly characteristic shapes. We might, for example, come across one that mathematicians would call "normal," or symmetrical around a midpoint:

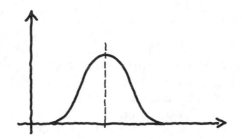

Far more common are skewed diagrams that look like this:

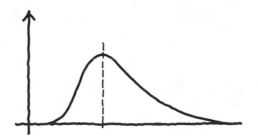

The reason for this is that human performance tends to be skewed in just this shape, with relatively more clustering at the high-performance end (usually the left, indicating quicker completion) than at the low-performance end.

Finally, there is a class of weird-looking diagrams such as the following:

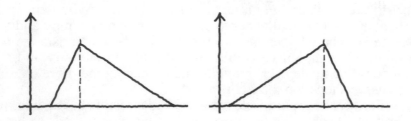

Weird, but useful. These rather artificial forms approximate smooth curves without sacrificing too much rigor. You can see the appeal of these triangular uncertainty diagrams: They allow us to focus on best case, worst case, and most likely case. As you will see, these curves are very handy for dealing with some of the component risks that drive our projects.

Aggregate and Causal Risks

So far, we've lumped together risks of two rather different types. We've given the risk profile of entire projects, expressed with uncertainty diagrams showing delivery dates, total cost or effort, or versions likely to be delivered by a fixed date. And we've also spoken of component risks, such as the production rate of staff or the loss of personnel. The first category consists of what we call *aggregate* risks, since they deal with the project as a whole; we call the second category *causal* or component risks. Clearly, the two are related. Uncertainty about an aggregate result is a direct function of the uncertainties in those causal factors that lead to success or failure:

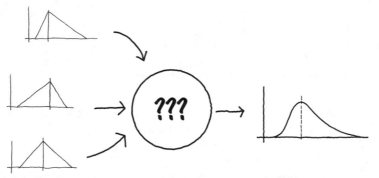

Causal Risks   **Aggregate Risks**

The process in the middle (the business of transforming a set of causal risks into aggregate risk) is what we refer to below as a "risk model."

As you can see, our prescription calls for the use of risk diagrams as input to and output from this process. In other words, each of the component or causal risks is described by a risk diagram, and we use an automated approach to digest the causals and to create from them an aggregate indicator of risk, again in the form of a diagram.

Two Kinds of Model

What would be handy here is a combination prognosticator and risk indicator. First, it would ask you for dozens or scores of questions about your project, and then it would put out a risk diagram showing a range of likely done dates, each of them associated with a degree of uncertainty. It would do your estimating for you and also perform an uncertainty analysis on the estimates it came up with.

Such a whizbang would be part parametric estimator and part uncertainty overlayer. The parametric estimator component of this is already available on the market. You probably already have such a tool, whether it was purchased by your company or developed in-house. You pour in what you know about the project (function points, SLIM parameters, COCOMO predictors, or whatever), together with some customizing information about your procedures and past history, and it offers up an elapsed time in which the project could be done.

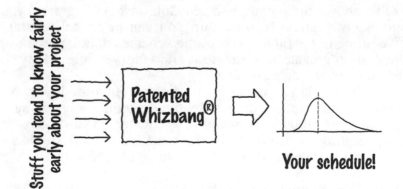

We're going to propose that you continue to use whatever your present estimator is (even if it's just a wet finger in the wind) and combine it with the risk model we supply in the two chapters just ahead. The estimator is your production model since it shows how much you can produce over time, and the risk model shows you how much uncertainty should be associated with the production estimate. Working together, the two models interact like this:

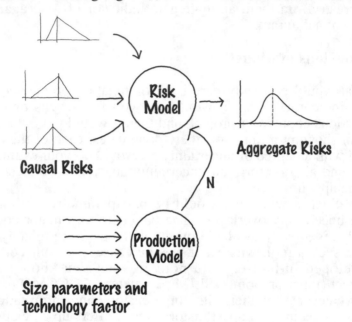

We've shown the output as a schedule in risk-diagram form. It shows how certain or uncertain you can be of delivery at any given time in the future. The same scheme could be used to produce an aggregate risk diagram showing versions likely to be delivered over a range of dates.

The single parameter connecting the two models is N, the nano-percent date. As implied by the diagram, we encourage you to turn your production model or estimator up to its most optimistic settings to determine N, the best case. The risk model then overlays the uncertainty to produce the aggregate diagram.

One More Nuance About Risk Diagrams

To demonstrate the next idea, we need to construct a very coarse uncertainty diagram (its coarseness will help the effect to be clearly visible).   Let's suppose we're studying a small group of students. We have some data about them, including their weight in pounds. We group the data points into twenty-pound increments and find that there is one child in the 101-to-120 pound group, three in the 121-to-140 pound group, and two in the 141-to-160 pound group:

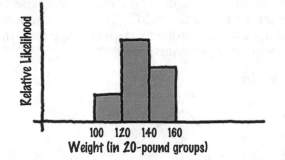

This graphic can be viewed as an uncertainty diagram: Suppose one of the kids is about to jump into your lap—this type of diagram can be used to show how uncertain you are about how much weight to expect. The diagram shows the relative likelihood of each of the three weight ranges.

The exact same data might be shown in a slightly different form, grouped cumulatively:

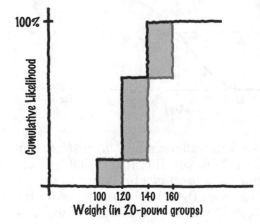

This diagram needs to be read slightly differently: The graph shows the probability that the child who jumps in your lap will be *in or below* the indicated weight group. Below the first weight group, the probability is zero (there are no kids who weigh less than 100 pounds in the class). At the upper weight group and beyond, the probability is 100 percent since all the kids in the class are in the top group or below.

Both diagrams portray the same data. The first shows the relative likelihood of there being a child in a given group, and the second shows the cumulative likelihood of there being a child in the indicated group or any lower one. We shall term these two kinds of uncertainty diagram *incremental* and *cumulative,* respectively.

Now, back to the real world: Shown below are the incremental risk diagram for a project's delivery date and, immediately underneath, its cumulative equivalent:

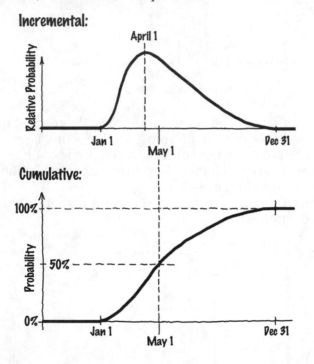

Again, both graphs show the same data, just presented slightly differently. The first thing you'll notice is that the scale along the vertical of the cumulative form is a bit easier to grasp: It conveys straight probability from 0 to 100 percent. Any date south of January 1 is hopeless (0-percent likely), and if we're willing to go all the way out to the end of December of next year, it's essentially certain (100-percent likely) that we'll make the date. The fact that May 1 of next year is the fifty-fifty date is read directly off the cumulative diagram, but you'd have to estimate areas to the left and right to see it on the incremental.

Both forms are useful, and if you have the data for either one, you can always use it to derive the other.

12

TOOLS AND PROCEDURES

Our two purposes in this chapter are (1) to provide you with a handy tool for assessing risks and (2) to give you some grounding in how to make use of it. The tool, called RISKOLOGY, is freely downloadable from our Website (http://www.systemsguild.com/riskology). It's a risk model in the sense described in the previous chapter. The tool is meant to be used in conjunction with your own production model or parametric estimator. Our tool will not estimate how long your project will take; all it will do is tell you how much uncertainty ought to be associated with whatever estimate you come up with.

The model is presented in the form of a spreadsheet. It comes with the logic needed to work with a set of quantified risks, as well as a starter database for four of the core risks of software development. (We discuss the core risks in Chapter 13.)

Just as you can drive a car without understanding all the intricacies of its motor and control systems, so too can you use the risk model without an insider's knowledge of how it works. In this chapter, though, we'll give you a peek inside the model. This will serve to demystify it a bit, and to give you a leg up if you decide to customize the spreadsheet to better match your own circumstances. Customization may be important because it enables you to eliminate at least some of the apparent uncertainty about your projects. Your locally collected data may be more optimistic and also more applicable than our industry-wide data.

Before we launch into the details, here's a promise to set your mind at ease: We haven't put any hairy mathematics into this chapter. If you can handle a bit of arithmetic, the chapter should be accessible to you. If you are up to using a spreadsheet to forecast your retirement income, for example, you shouldn't have any trouble taking the risk model apart and putting it back together, in case you decide to customize it.

Complex Mixing

At the heart of any risk model is a technique for determining the combined effect of two or more uncertainties:

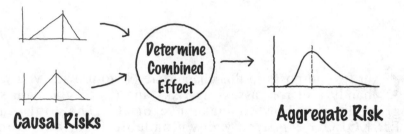

Toward the end of the next chapter, we'll show how this works for software projects. Right here, though, we're going to demonstrate the concept on an admittedly contrived problem that's a bit easier to grasp.

Let's say that you're a runner. You jog every day, faithfully, but vary the time depending on your other commitments. Your daily workout takes anywhere from fifteen minutes to nearly an hour. You keep records and find that, fairly independent of distance (within this time range), your running speed varies from six-and-a-half to nine miles an hour. You've done this for so long that you have a respectable record:

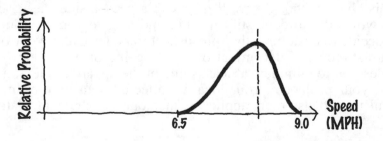

The actual data was probably in the form of a bar chart; what we've shown here is the envelope curve that approximates that bar chart. This looks like an uncertainty diagram, and that's exactly what it is. In fact, it can be presented in the two usual forms, as shown below:

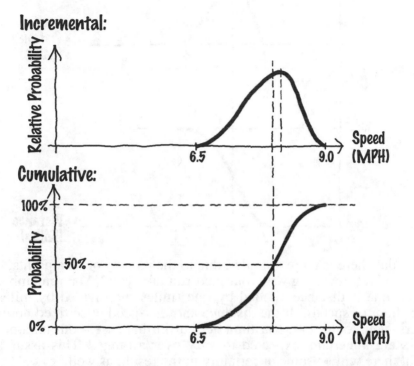

This distribution of past results can be seen as a representation of uncertainty about how fast you'll run the next time out.

Suppose your speed is not the only uncertainty affecting your next run. Suppose you've decided to run around a path of unknown length: the perimeter of a golf course. Since you've never run there before, you're not at all sure just how long a run it will be. You do have some data, however, from the Professional Golfers' Association, about course perimeters, telling you that the distance around the courses varies from two to four miles, with the most likely perimeter at approximately 2.8 miles. This, too, can be expressed as a distribution:

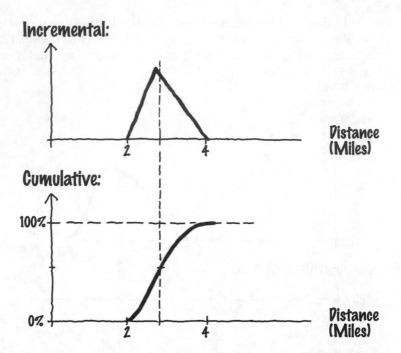

The data here is more granular, due to the paucity of data points.

Now, how long will your next run take you? You remember that time is distance divided by rate (miles run divided by miles per hour of speed). If the distance and the speed were fixed numbers, you could do the arithmetic, but in this case, both parameters are uncertain, expected to vary over a range. This assures that there will be some uncertainty in the result, as well:

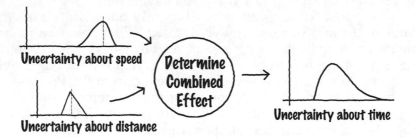

In order to *derive* the output curve that is the composite of the two input curves, we would need to adopt a method from integral calculus. But such hairy mathematics is not allowed in this chapter. So, what can we do?

Instead of deriving the curve, we're going to *approximate* it by simulating a series of successive runs. To achieve this, we'll need to build a sampling tool that gives us a series of sample data points from any uncertainty pattern, while at the same time guaranteeing to respect the shape of the pattern over time. Such a tool applied to the speed diagram would look like this:

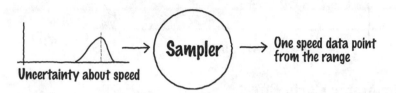

If you were the sampler in this case, how would you proceed? Delivering the first point is easy; you look over the spread from minimum to maximum and come up with any point in between. Who can fault you, no matter what number you come up with? But if you have to do this more than once, the requirement that you "respect the shape of the pattern over time" gives you pause. How do you deliver a series of data points that respects the spread of possibilities exactly as shown in the original uncertainty diagram?

However you do it, the pattern of delivered data points will have to eventually replicate the uncertainty diagram of the input. To check yourself, you might want to collect your results over time—pigeonholed into convenient groupings—and use them to produce a bar chart of your sampled outputs. If you've correctly figured out the sampling process, successive bar charts (for more and more samples) might look like this:

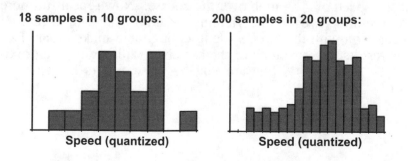

Eventually, once you have a few hundred data points, the envelope containing your bar chart will look pretty much like the uncertainty diagram you started out with:

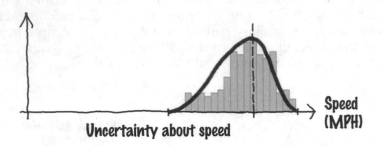

The Monte Carlo Effect

Monte Carlo sampling is an approach that guarantees to respect the shape of the observed pattern over time. A Monte Carlo sampler makes use of past observed data, in the form of a cumulative uncertainty diagram, together with a simple random number generator that picks samples. If you pick enough of them, the bar chart of samples will begin to approximate the pattern of your observed data. The generator is configured to produce random numbers between zero and one. The trick is to use each generated number to pick a value along the vertical of the uncertainty diagram and to draw a horizontal line across. If the first generated number is .312, for example, you draw a horizontal line at .312 on the vertical axis (see the top graph on the next page).

You then draw a vertical line through the point where your horizontal intersects the curve. The value read from the horizontal axis is your first sample point (see the bottom graph on the next page).

The second graph says that for the first sample run, you can expect a speed of 7.66 mph over the course. Now repeat for more random numbers, each one yielding a sample value of speed. If you carry on with this process long enough and make a bar chart of the results, the envelope of the bar chart will begin to approximate the uncertainty diagram you began with (its incremental form).

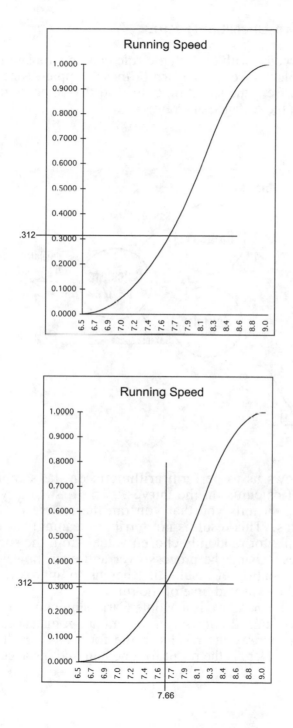

Simulating the Two-Uncertainty Run

The sampler constructed with this simple rule can now be applied to the running problem. We'll need two of these samplers, one to give us data points from the speed diagram and the other to give us data points from the distance diagram:

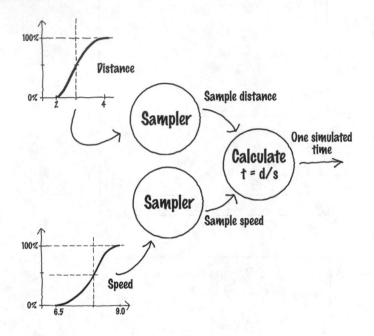

This approach allows us to perform arithmetic on the samples instead of integral calculus on the curves. The first time you invoke this process, it tells you that you ran the course in, for example, 33 minutes. This result is not terribly meaningful—it's just a calculated time for randomly chosen values from the speed and distance ranges. Using the process over and over, however, will produce a distribution of results that begins to approximate the uncertainty in the expected time of the run.

The diagram shown above is a Monte Carlo simulator for the two-uncertainty problem. It allows you to simulate *n* instances of the problem and to portray the results in the form of a resultant uncertainty diagram. Here is the result for one hundred instances:

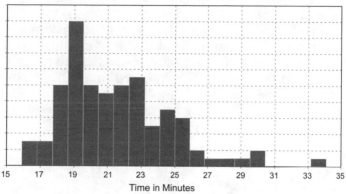

Simulation Results: Time Around P.G.A. Course

Time in Minutes

The technique used here is not limited to two uncertainties. It can be used for an entire portfolio of the risks plaguing a software project.

The Software Project Risk Model

RISKOLOGY is a Monte Carlo simulator that we created for the software risk manager. It is a straightforward implementation of Monte Carlo sampling, expressed in spreadsheet logic. We've written it in Excel, so you'll need a legal copy of the program to make use of the tool. RISKOLOGY comes packaged with our own data about some of the risks likely to be facing your project. You can use our data or override with your own.

Download a copy of the RISKOLOGY simulator from our Website:

http://www.systemsguild.com/riskology

Also available there are some templates and instructions for using and customizing the simulator.

A Side-Effect of Using Simulation

Once you've simulated sufficient instances of your project, the simulator will provide you with an acceptably smooth output curve. The curve can be made to show the aggregate risks around your project delivery date or around delivered functionality as of a fixed end date. In risk management terms, the result is conveyed as an aggregate risk diagram.

For people who are not in the know about risk management, or for those who have particular difficulty grappling with uncertainty, we suggest that you present it instead as the result of simulation. "We ran this project five hundred times in the simulator," you might say, "and the result is this":

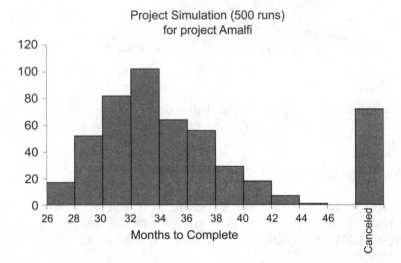

"As you can see," you say, "it shows us delivering before the end of Month 30 only about 15 percent of the time. That doesn't mean the date is impossible, only that it's risky. You can count on it with only a 15-percent confidence factor. If you wanted a 75-percent confidence factor, you'd be better off advertising a delivery date in Month 40."

Alternatives to RISKOLOGY

Our RISKOLOGY simulator is not your only option. There are similar products available for sale. Rather than provide direct pointers here, we will maintain a set at the RISKOLOGY Website (see the URL above). Also described there are at least two meta-risk tools—kits for building your own risk simulators. These products are inexpensive and fairly easily mastered.

Next, as promised, we turn to what we consider the most common, core risks faced by those who run software projects.

13

CORE RISKS OF
SOFTWARE PROJECTS

If you've been in the software business for any time at all, you know that there are certain common problems that plague one project after another. Missed schedules and creeping requirements are not things that just happen to you once and then go away, never to appear again. Rather, they are part of the territory. We all know that. What's odd is that we don't plan our projects as if we knew it. Instead, we plan as if our past problems are locked in the past and will never rear their ugly heads again. Of course, you know that isn't a reasonable expectation. This chapter will help you figure out how much your next project plan needs to accommodate the problems you've observed in the past. While we're at it, we'll demonstrate use of the RISKOLOGY simulator as a tool for applying patterns of core risk behavior to a new project plan.

Risks Common to All Software Projects

You could probably make a list of twenty or thirty problems that are so ubiquitous they could reasonably be expected to appear—at least to some extent—on every project. We've chosen to work with only five. We selected these five because they account for most of the deviation between plan and actual, and also because we have been able to collect some useful industry data on the extent of these risks. Here's our shortlist of core risks:

1. inherent schedule flaw
2. requirements inflation (requirements creep)
3. employee turnover
4. specification breakdown
5. poor productivity

Of these, only the last is really performance-related. The other four are almost totally independent of how hard you work and how competent and clever you are about doing that work. This is worth emphasizing because one of the worries many managers have about risk management is that it will be an excuse for poor performance. But making some reasonable provision for these uncontrollables is the heart of risk management. Such a provision doesn't give you leave to fail; it just sets aside a reserve in case some number of these uncontrollables turn against you.

The following sections define the five risks and show industry patterns to quantify them.

Core Risk #1: Schedule Flaw

The first core risk is due to some flaw in—or the total bankruptcy of—the process of setting budgets for time and effort. This can be viewed as an error in the schedule itself as opposed to an error in the way the project is run. (That overaggressiveness can be a schedule flaw will come as a surprise to the kind of managers who have never seen an aggressive schedule they didn't like.) Schedule flaw is not only a real risk; it is the largest of the five core risks in its impact on plan versus actual performance.

Schedule flaw can be viewed as a tendency to misjudge the size of the product to be built. If you make a serious effort to size a software product—let's say in function points or COCOMO-weighted KLOC, or the equivalent—there is still a serious likelihood of undersizing. You're more inclined to neglect work that turns out to be needed than to include work that subsequently proves unnecessary. Any oversizing that happens to be in your plan is seldom sufficient to offset the undersizing.

If you *don't* make a serious effort to size the product, then your schedule estimates are based on nothing more than wishful thinking: "Gee, the customer wants this by May; May is seven months away, so I guess the schedule is seven months." When the schedule is set without regard to product size, overruns of 50 to 80 percent are likely. When a seven-month project ends up taking twelve months, angry upper managers seldom blame the schedule; instead, they blame those who were supposed to make that schedule—no matter how ridiculous it was—into reality. But the problem is flawed schedule, not flawed performance. In retrospect, the product was undersized by fiat; the act of restricting the length of the project limited its size to what could be built in that time, and that limit turned out to be unrealistic.

How big a problem is schedule flaw across the software industry? In order to come up with an answer to this, we had to digest overrun data, including data that others had collected, and then back out the effects of the remaining core risks. This enabled us to assert that we had isolated the effect of schedule flaw. This separation of causal factors is not a trivial problem— and we don't claim to have achieved perfection in our result—but the following uncertainty diagram is our best assessment of deviation from schedule due, on average, to improper scheduling alone:

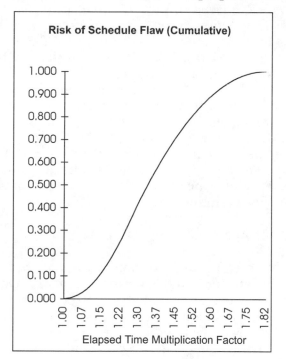

As the graph implies, if we know nothing else about your project or your organization, our safest bet is that your original size estimate—either directly calculated or inferred by a fiat schedule—

will cause you to overrun your schedule by at least 30 percent. For example, a horizontal drawn at 0.50 intersects the curve at a point implying 1.30 or more of a time-multiplication factor.

The situation shown here is considerably worse than it needs to be. The industry-wide trend is compromised by the fact that so many companies don't do their homework on sizing, opting instead for backward scheduling or pure wishful thinking. While we as an industry do no better than the pattern shown in the graph above, those companies that do make a serious effort to size can reduce the impact of schedule flaw to less than 15 percent. Collecting data for a few projects on the extent of undersizing could teach you to set aside a sensible provision for this on future projects. Eventually, you could produce a risk diagram that was balanced, where the fifty-fifty point is at 0-percent overrun and the likelihood of finishing ahead of schedule (considering this one core risk alone) is equal to the likelihood of finishing late.

Our data is biased toward smallish projects, those under three-thousand function points. Larger projects seem to suffer slightly less from this effect. Maybe fewer of them try to bypass the sizing effort. Also, larger (longer) projects afford greater opportunity for resizing along the way.

We asserted above that most of the core risks had no implication of poor performance by the team. This is true of the schedule-flaw risk, but only if we ignore the performance of management. Managers who come up with or agree to seriously flawed schedule commitments are performing poorly. The key point is that when a project overruns its schedule, it is in spite of, not due to, developer performance. The team, apart from the manager, may be performing at an optimal level.

Core Risk #2: Requirements Inflation

The piece of software that you and your staff build is always intended to fit into somebody's business domain. One thing you can be sure of is that the domain is not going to remain static during the building process. It will change at a rate dictated by its markets and its own invention rate. If you set out in January to deliver an X, ten months hence, by the end of those ten months, an X is no longer what your business partners really want. What they really want is an X-prime. The difference between what they wanted at the beginning and what they want at the end is due to some change that has affected the domain in the meantime.

From the project's point of view, this change is always inflation. Even removing something already built is a kind of inflation since it causes increased work.

How much inflation should you reasonably expect? If you agree with what we've written in the last two paragraphs, you can see that 0 percent is not a good answer. Yet it is the answer implied by the way we usually schedule new projects. Our reasoning seems to go,

> *If you want an X, we can give it to you in ten months; if you turn out to want something other than an X, that's your problem.*

But it isn't. Hitting the moving target is everybody's problem. Planning on delivering in the future exactly what the stakeholders say that they want today is like throwing a football to where the receiver used to be.

A better logic would go something like this: "You say you want an X; our experience suggests that there will be some change in that requirement along the way and that you will eventually end up wanting something slightly different, so we will plan on building an X with some accommodation for expected change."

But how much? In the mid 1990's, the U.S. Department of Defense (DoD) proposed some quantitative targets for how well-run projects should behave. They quantified the extent of reasonably expected change to be something less than 1 percent per month. So, a project that set out to build a product sized at twenty-thousand function points, over two years, should expect to build about twenty-five thousand function points of software (20,000fp * (1.00 + 24 months * 1% per month)). The actual deliverable may be sized somewhere in between since some of the changes will cause work already completed and paid for to be discarded.

The DoD experience may be somewhat difficult to apply to your project. Since typical DoD software products are large, the projects are contracted and sometimes subcontracted to several levels, and the projects are longer than most commercial efforts. Furthermore, the DoD approximation is expressed in terms of size itself rather than the time effect of changing size.

From our own data—which is rich in one- and two-year projects with ten or fewer staff members—we come up with the following expected time effect of shifting requirements:

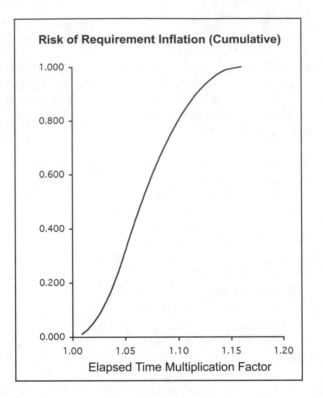

The impact of this risk may be different in your organization from what we have shown. Of course, you'll want to override our data with your own, if you have any (see the next section for tips on overriding). If you don't have data, use what we've provided in the RISKOLOGY simulator as a starting point. It is sure to be a better guess than the standard one of expecting 0-percent change.

Core Risk #3: Turnover

People sometimes leave during a project. The possibility that this will happen is usually left out of the estimation process. To take account of this factor, you'll want to allocate some buffer to contain the risk. How much? This is what we come up with from our project database:

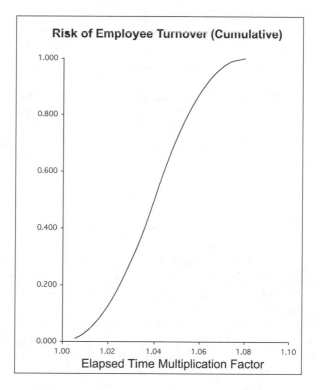

Shown here is the effect of employee turnover on one- and two-year projects, assuming industry average turnover figures.

This is one core risk for which you are likely to have decent internal data, and you should override our risk table with one of your own. The instructions for overriding are available at the RISKOLOGY Website. The information you'll need to complete your override is this:

- average turnover percentage per year for technical staff at your company
- your own best assessment of *ramp-up time* for each replacement hired

We define ramp-up time as the number of months it takes a typical new hire to begin performing at the level of the person he or she replaces. Figures for ramp-up time tend to vary from around two months for a plain-vanilla in-house business IT shop to twenty-four months for companies doing esoteric engineering applications. Obviously, the extent of ramp-up time is a function of how complex your domain is and how much it deviates from the norm (from the kind of experience base your typical new hire might have).

Coming up with a reasonable assessment of ramp-up time may be a chore, but any well-thought-out number you come up with is a great improvement on zero, the default assumption that has always been built into our project management hypothesis set . . . until now.

Core Risk #4: Specification Breakdown

The fourth core risk, specification breakdown, is different in kind from the others. It is discrete rather than continuous, binary in its effect (in other words, it either happens or doesn't happen, rather than affecting you to some varying degree), and when it does happen, it is almost always fatal. It doesn't slow your project down—it sinks it.

Specification breakdown refers to the collapse of the negotiation process that is at the heart of requirements-setting, at the beginning of any project. You might think that this would be a relatively easy problem to spot, and therefore fairly containable: The various parties just can't agree on what product to build, so you cancel early, pick up your marbles, and go home without too great a loss.

Unfortunately, it seldom works that way. People are *supposed* to agree. They are *supposed* to cooperate. When there is sufficiently deep conflict to make that impossible, the effect is often covered up. The project goes ahead with a flawed, ambiguous target, something that no one is happy with but that each party can live with for the time being, at least.

Let's say that the conflict is over which stakeholder is to control a certain key piece of data. The specification artfully avoids stating where the data is to reside, what permissions are required to alter it, what audits track it, which backup it is part of, whether it is altered by certain transactions, when and how it can be overridden, and so on. People grumble over the spec because it isn't very clear. But it also has the advantage of not being clearly unacceptable to any of the parties. The project proceeds (or seems to proceed) into internal design and implementation activities.

The covered-up problem goes away for a time, but not permanently. While it is possible to *specify* a product ambiguously, it is not possible to *build* a product ambiguously. Eventually, the deferred problems need to be faced, and the conflict arises again. In the worst cases, this happens very late in the project, after most or all of the budgeted time and money have been used up. The project is fragile at that point, and erosion of support by any of the parties can lead to a quick cancellation. The project is effectively killed without anyone ever needing to confess to the underlying lack of accord that was the real problem.

Specification breakdown manifests itself in other ways as well. One of these is what management authority Peter Keen calls counter-implementation, in which disaffected stakeholders overload the project with more and more functionality.[1] Functions A through F are used to justify a project. But then functions G through Z are added on by seemingly enthusiastic supporters of the project. With that much added functionality, there is no hope of benefit exceeding cost. This kind of "piling on" typically happens late in the analysis activity and results in a failure to close on specification.

About a seventh of all the projects in our database were canceled without delivering anything. Other researchers have come up with different estimates of the proportion of canceled projects, but most are in the range of 10 to 15 percent. We've taken a middle value from this percentage range of project cancellations and treated it as a fixed specification-breakdown risk. For simplicity, we have assumed that specification breakdown is the only cause of project cancellation. (You can probably find a project somewhere that was canceled for reasons having nothing to do with stakeholder conflict; be sure, though, that the purported reason is not just a cover up for a deep lack of accord among the parties.)

The application of this core risk is also a bit unique. We propose that you burden each new project with this cancellation risk up until there is clear closure on specification. After that, you turn the risk off.

To deal with the problem of ambiguity used to conceal disagreement, we define specification closure to mean that all parties sign off on the boundary data going into and out of the product, and on definitions down to the data element level of all dataflows arriving or departing from the software to be constructed. Notice that this agreement is only on data, not on functions to be performed

---

[1]Peter G.W. Keen, "Information Systems and Organizational Change," *Communications of the ACM,* Vol. 24, No. 1 (January 1981), pp. 24–33.

on that data or functions required in order to produce the data. While agreement on dataflows may only be part of the required accord, it is a key part. Since data descriptions are less prone to ambiguity than function descriptions, we feel safe concluding that sign-off on net arriving and departing dataflows is a fair indicator of accord. When such an accord is reached, the cancellation risk should be deactivated.

There is some pseudo-science here that ought not to be allowed to stand unchallenged. We've ignored additional causes of cancellation and produced our RISKOLOGY simulator so that it forces you to confront the possibility of project cancellation up until our sign-off milestone is met—and then it shows zero chance of cancellation from that point on. This is a fairly coarse handling of the delicate matter of canceled projects, justified only by the fact that such a high proportion of the projects that eventually get canceled never can muster the agreement necessary to pass the milestone.

Core Risk #5: Under-Performance

There is a lot of evidence in the literature of substantial differences in performance across any population of developers. The differences among whole project teams are damped somewhat and always less than the extremes of difference between individuals. Further, some of the difference in individual performance is due to one or another of the four core risks that we've already presented. After backing out the effect of the other risks and spreading individual differences across teams, we come up with this effect of team performance variation (see graph, below).

This factor tends to be fairly balanced: You are essentially as likely to get a positive break on performance as a negative one.

There is a danger in using our data for very small teams since individual differences there may not damp out. A team of one, for example, exposes you to a far greater effect of under- or over-performance.

A balanced risk such as under/over-performance merely introduces noise into the process. It widens your window of uncertainty without shifting mean expectation in either direction.

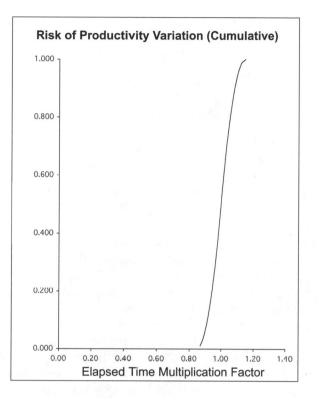

Combined Effect of the Core Risks

The simulator asks you for a few project parameters, gives you the opportunity to override any or all of the core risks with your own data, and then runs instances of the project to profile how long it can be expected to take. The profile is the result of five-hundred separate simulations, with finish dates grouped into dis-crete ranges. For a project (here named Amalfi) with N at about 26 months and no overrides, the RISKOLOGY simulation results look like the figure you encountered at the end of Chapter 12:

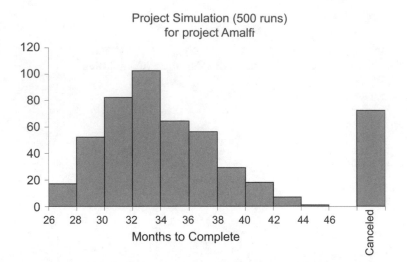

Project Simulation (500 runs)
for project Amalfi

If this were your project, here's how you might interpret and explain the result: There is some nonzero likelihood of delivering your product in the period from Month 26 to Month 27. It's far more likely, however, that you'll be done by Months 32 to 34. For a 75-percent confidence level, you may have to go all the way out to Month 38. About 15 percent of the runs ended up with the project being canceled. That is a fair assessment of the cancellation risk, looking forward at the project from day one, but within the first six months, it should be possible to assess that cancellation risk much more precisely and perhaps retire it.

Core Risks as an Indicator of Completeness

Core risks can also be used to assess whether or not the risk management process has been reasonably performed. For example, if you represent the five core risks but use different data from ours, you may still reasonably assert that you've done risk management and done it sensibly. We take a very dim view, however, of projects that claim to be managing risks when they have clearly not taken account of these five core risks.

14

A DEFINED PROCESS FOR RISK DISCOVERY

Core risks are not the only ones you need to worry about. There may well be risks particular to your project that have to be figured into your risk equation. For example, there may be one key player whose departure could be disastrous to the project, an important user who might defect and choose to go his own way, or a vendor whose nonperformance could have ugly consequences.

Once you've identified and quantified these risks, they can be managed just like the others. But getting them out on the table can be a problem. The culture of our organizations sometimes makes it impossible to talk about a really worrisome risk. We are like a primitive tribe that tries to hold the devil at bay by refusing to say his name.

Keeping mum about a risk won't make it go away. The staff of the Ariane 5 project,[1] for example, never did articulate the risk that a compiler would do no boundary checking, and thus compromise the launch vehicle. It happened anyway and resulted in the total failure of the launch.

The bread-and-butter act of risk discovery is someone saying, "You know, if <whatever> happened, we'd really be up the creek. . . ." Usually, the person has known about the risk for a

---

[1] Ariane 5 was the European Space Agency's satellite launch that blew up due to a software error in 1996.

while, and may even have done a private assessment on it, something in the form of, "I'd better get my résumé polished up if it
starts to look like <whatever> might happen." When the only risk
management on a project is happening inside the head of a single
worried individual, that suggests a breakdown in communication.
Specifically, it usually means there are disincentives at work,
stopping the flow of essential information.

Naming the Disincentives

Let's think about these disincentives within a real context: On the
morning of January 28, 1986, the *Challenger* spacecraft exploded,
with devastating loss of life and treasure and national prestige.
The ensuing investigation revealed that the extended cold snap
leading up to the launch caused the entire first stage rocket and all
its components to be out of specified temperature range. The
system was meant to operate at temperatures above freezing, and
it was clearly colder than that. No one on the staff was thinking
about O-rings, but a great many people knew that components of
the system were temperature-sensitive and could not be counted
on to perform to spec at subfreezing temperatures. Why didn't
they speak up?

Their reasons were the same ones that stop people from
articulating risks at companies everywhere. They take the form of
unwritten rules, built into the corporate culture:

1. Don't be a negative thinker.
2. Don't raise a problem unless you have a solution for it.
3. Don't say something is a problem unless you can *prove*
    it is.
4. Don't be the spoiler.
5. Don't articulate a problem unless you want its imme-
    diate solution to become your responsibility.

Healthy cultures attach great value to the concept of a team. Being
judged a "team player" is enormously important, and not being
one can be fatal to a career. Articulating a risk shouldn't be seen
as anti-team, but it often is. These unwritten rules are not very dis-
criminating. They don't make much distinction between speaking
up responsibly and whining. And because the rules are never discussed openly, they never get adjusted for changing circumstances.

We are all enjoined to adopt a can-do mentality in our work.
And there's the rub. Saying the name of a risk is an exercise in

can't-do. Risk discovery is profoundly at odds with this funda-
mental aspect of our organizations.

Since the disincentives are powerful, we need an open, fixed,
and well-understood process to make it possible to speak. We
need a ritual, a way for all to participate fully while still remaining
safe. At the heart of the ritual are some temporary rules that make
it okay—for the moment, at least—to disobey the unwritten rules.
If your boss specifically asks you in public to "be the devil's advocate about this idea," you are clearly excused from the dictates of
can-do thinking. That will make it acceptable for you to indulge
in negative, what-if thinking. This is just what our defined process
for risk discovery has to achieve.

The Defined Process

The defined process that we propose involves working backward
in three steps to identify risks:

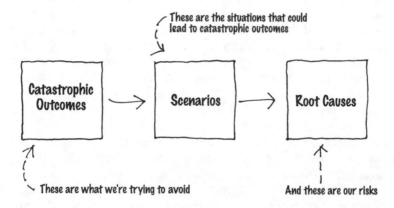

When an actual catastrophe happens, these three steps occur in
the opposite order, moving from cause to unfolding scenario to
resulting outcome. But it is too threatening to deal with them in
this temporal order. Working backward is less scary. It lets you
focus first on the possible nightmare outcome, pretty much in isolation, divorced from cause. Even so, it's still not easy for people
to express such fears:

TRL: Last year, I had to have arthroscopic knee surgery,
       involving complete anesthesia. The night before I went
       into the hospital, my wife asked me if I was anxious
       about the surgery. I quickly responded that I was not,

that thousands of these operations occur with no problems at all. After a while, I did admit to her that I had what I considered a bit of an irrational fear. I was worried that the surgeon would operate on the wrong knee. My wife told me to tell him that. The next morning, I was prepped for surgery and my wife was keeping me company. The surgeon came in to tell us about the post-surgery procedures. My wife was looking at me, with eyebrows arched. I said nothing. Just before the surgeon went off for his preparations, he took out a marker pen and wrote, "YES," on my thigh, just above the knee about to be operated on. My wife smiled; we all smiled.

The ritual has to make it okay to share fears. If the doctor had explicitly asked Tim in the pre-op room what his worst fear was, the matter would have been quickly out on the table. The ritual has to ask all participants to share their worst fears. Sometimes it helps to be allowed to say (as Tim said above) that the fear is irrational.

The rest of the process is to deduce how such a nightmare could come about. The trick is to make the three steps more or less mechanical, involving no question of blame. "My nightmare is this; here is a scenario that could result in precisely that nightmare; and the thing that might kick off such a scenario is . . ." Voilà, one risk identified.

To undo the mojo of the unwritten rules, the risk-discovery process needs to be written down and distributed before the event begins. You can't spring it on people and expect them to suspend the unwritten rules without a good, formal cover.

The risk-discovery process should not happen just once, at the beginning of the project. There has to be some commitment to make it a continuing part of the project review. At each risk-discovery meeting, there has to be a formal statement of the approach to be followed, so that unwritten rules are effectively suspended.

The three steps typically happen together, at the same meeting. But, the techniques are unique to each step, so it's worth going over each in turn.

Step 1: Catastrophe Brainstorm

A brainstorm is a contrived group-invention experience. The idea is to use group dynamics to find ways around conventional thinking and to let fresh new thoughts emerge. A catastrophe brainstorm is slightly different, but most of the techniques of classical brainstorming are useful. For a good description of these techniques, look into the brainstorming section in the References.

Brainstorming makes use of *ploys,* little tricks to help the group get past its inevitable blocks and dead moments. The titles listed in the References provide dozens of these ploys, all of them useful in getting the group to think up meaningful nightmares. A few ploys that are unique to catastrophe brainstorms are presented below:

1. *Frame the question explicitly in terms of a nightmare:* For some reason, this also helps undo the effect of the unwritten rules; no matter how positive-thinking the culture may be, it's still okay to wake up at night with an awful thought. Ask people what their worst fears are for the project. When they wake up in a sweat over the project, what is it that upset them?
2. *Use a crystal ball:* Pretend you have access to a crystal ball, or the ability to conjure up headlines from next year's newspaper. Assert that this glimpse into the future shows disaster for the project, but what disaster? Or say the company has been profiled in *The Wall Street Journal*'s idiot column (in the middle of the front page) for the awful way the project turned out. Now ask, "How could that have happened?"
3. *Switch perspectives:* Ask people to describe their best dreams for the project, and then discuss an inverted version of those dreams.
4. *Ask about blame-free disasters:* How could the project fail without it really being anybody's fault?
5. *Ask about blameworthy failure:* Ask people, "How could the project go spectacularly awry and have it be our fault? the user's fault? management's fault? your fault?" (This only works if you make sure to get everybody into the act.)

6. *Imagine partial failure:* Ask how the project might succeed in general but leave one particular stakeholder
unsatisfied or angry.

Brainstorms are fast and furious, so you'll need to make some
provision for capturing all the suggestions. Make sure that the
facilitator is not the one responsible for capture.

Step 2: Scenario-Building

Now go back over the captured catastrophes one by one, and
imagine together one or more scenarios that might lead to each
result. Scenario imagining can be fairly mechanical, but the question of blame may be hanging in the air—so expect some tension
here. Again, a capture mechanism needs to be thought out and
implemented in advance so that suddenly increased tension won't
result in losing the very issues that need attention most.

It's worth attaching at least a tentative probability to these
scenarios. Obviously, the highly improbable ones are less valuable since they won't justify the effort of being carried further.
Be suspicious, though, of the low probability that the group may
attach to a given scenario; someone offered it, and to that
someone, it probably wasn't a negligible matter.

In lieu of doing probability analysis on the spot, you might
defer it to be done later by a subgroup. This will allow some
empirical evidence to make the case that a given scenario is or is
not worth worrying about.

Step 3: Root Cause Analysis

With a scenario in front of your group, it's possible for everyone
to work together to figure out potential root causes. This is much
easier to do before the scenario has actually begun. When the
scenario is only an abstraction—that is, some stupid thing that
might happen—it's possible to imagine causes without assigning
blame: "Well, I can't imagine this happening unless some idiot
stole staff members to put out fires elsewhere." That's easy
enough to say—even if the potential idiot is in the room—before
the catastrophe has actually happened.

Your risks are the root causes of scenarios that will likely
lead to catastrophic outcomes.

Root cause analysis is harder than it looks. The reason for this is not just the effect of the unwritten rule base, but the complex notion of "rootness." (How root is root enough?) This is a process that is better performed by a group than by individuals in isolation. For useful tips on conducting root cause analysis sessions, consult the root cause analysis section in the References.

The WinWin Alternative

Barry Boehm's WinWin Spiral Process Model brings together much of that admirable man's career accomplishments to date. (See the References or the RISKOLOGY Website for links.) It integrates

- the spiral development life cycle
- metrics (specifically COCOMO II)
- risk management
- "theory W" of group interaction

It is a recipe for running sensible IT projects in light of the kinds of problems that typically dog such endeavors.

Boehm's unique approach to software development is worth knowing about for reasons that go beyond the scope of this book. Our purpose in mentioning it here, however, is to describe one minor aspect of WinWin that casts a useful light on risk discovery.

In WinWin, the project makes an up-front commitment to seek out all stakeholders and solicit from each one the so-called win conditions that would make the project a success from his or her point of view. In this methodology, the requirement is defined as the set of win conditions. Nothing can be considered a requirement if no one can be found to identify it as one of his or her win conditions. Sometimes there are conflicts among win conditions, particularly as the set of stakeholders grows. A win condition expressed by one party may make it difficult or impossible to achieve win conditions expressed by one or more of the other parties. Under WinWin, any pair of win conditions with conflict or tension between them represents a risk.

You may be able to use Boehm's trick to uncover risks that might never be discovered in any other fashion. So many of the risks that plague IT projects are directly due to conflicting win conditions, and the WinWin approach to risk discovery goes right to the heart of this root cause. Even if your project does not do a formal and complete solicitation of win conditions, you owe it to yourself to do some WinWin thinking as part of risk discovery. Think of it as one of the ploys you utilize. Ask participants, "Can you think of an obvious win condition for this project that is in conflict with somebody's win condition?" Each identified conflict is a potential risk.

15

RISK MANAGEMENT DYNAMICS

Despite a few repeated assertions on our part that risk management needs to be an ongoing activity, you might still have the sense that it happens at the beginning of a project and then (aside from an occasional bit of lip service) goes quietly to sleep till the next project.

Perfectly prescient beings might be able to go about risk management that way, but not us. When projects go awry, they often do so at or near the midpoint, so that's where risk management needs to be particularly active. The cause of problems almost always arises earlier than that, but the perception of the problems begins around mid-project: The early project activities seem to have gone swimmingly, and then everything falls apart. This is a project stage that we might label Comeuppance: the revisiting upon us of our past sins, including poor planning, overlooked tasks, imperfectly nurtured relationships, hidden assumptions, overreliance on good luck, and so on.

In this chapter, we address the role of risk management at and around the Comeuppance period, through to the end of the project.

Risk Management from Comeuppance On

Here is our quick list of risk management activities that need to be kept active through the project's middle stages and on, all the way to the end:

1. continuous monitoring of transition indicators, looking for anything on the risk list that seems close to switching from Only An Ugly Possibility to Legitimate Problem
2. ongoing risk discovery
3. data collection to feed the risk repository (database of the quantified impact of past observed problems)
4. daily tracking of closure metrics (see below)

Items 1 and 2 were treated in Chapters 9 and 14 and will not be described further here. Items 3 and 4 both have to do with metrics: quantitative indications of project size, scope, complexity, and state. These metrics are the subject of this chapter and the next.

Closure Metrics

We've used the phrase *closure metric* here to refer to a particular class of state metric, one that indicates the state of project completeness. A perfect closure metric (if only some perfect ones existed) would give you a firm 0-percent done indication at the beginning of the project and a 100-percent done indication at the end. In between, it would provide monotonically increasing values in the range of zero to one hundred. In the best of all worlds, postmortem analysis of the project would later conclude that the value of the perfect closure metric at each stage of the project had been a clean and clear predictor of time and effort remaining.

Granted, there are no perfect closure metrics, but there are some imperfect ones that can be incredibly useful. Two that we advocate are

*   boundary elements closure
*   earned value running (EVR)

These metrics give us a way to monitor the five core risks that we laid out in Chapter 13. The first is a metric to protect specifically against the core risk of specification breakdown. And the second is a general indicator of net progress, used to track the impact of the other four core risks.

Boundary Elements Closure

A system is a means of transforming inputs into outputs, as shown in the following diagram:

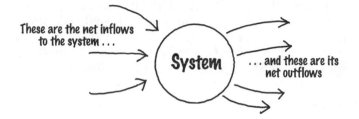

This is a fair description, whether the system we're talking about is a government agency, an accountancy firm, a typical IT system, the human liver or spleen, . . . essentially anything that we're inclined to call "a system."

IT systems are different in this sense: They are transformations of data inputs into data outputs. Traditionally, the business of specifying such systems has focused almost entirely on defining their transformation rules, the policies and approaches the system must implement in converting its inputs into outputs. Often overlooked in the specification process is a rigorous and detailed description of the net flows themselves, in and out. There are some compelling reasons for this omission: The work of defining these flows tends to be viewed as a design task, something left for the programmers to work on at a later stage. And it can also be time-consuming. Delaying the full definition makes good sense for projects that are destined to succeed, but there is a set of less fortunate projects in which detailed definition of the net flows will never succeed because it will call into stark relief certain conflicts in the stakeholder community. The existence of these flawed projects causes us to push the activity of net-flow definition backward in the life cycle, making it an early project deliverable. Our intention is to force conflict to surface early, rather than allow it to be papered over in the early project stages, only to crop up later.

In this approach, the net boundary flows are defined, but not designed. By that, we mean they are decomposed down to the data element level but not yet packaged in any kind of layout. The purpose of doing this work early is to require a sign-off by all parties on the makeup of net flows. In most projects, the sign-off can be obtained within the first 15 percent of project duration. When no sign-off is forthcoming and the project is clearly beyond the 15-percent point, this is a clear indication of either conflict in the stakeholder community (no viable consensus on what system to build) or a woeful misestimate of project duration. In either case, the missing sign-off represents a manifested risk, and a key one. There is no use working on anything else until boundary-elements closure can be obtained. If it can't be obtained, there is no better option available than project cancellation.

EVR (First Pass)

Earned value running is a metric of project doneness. Its purpose is to tell you how far along you've come on the journey from 0-percent done to 100-percent done.

Because EVR is tied tightly to a project's approach to incremental construction, we've chosen to defer the detailed definition of the metric to our discussion on incrementalism in the next chapter. In this first pass over the subject, we'll show only the basic intention of the metric and its relationship to the incremental version plan.

Suppose we look inside the system you've set out to build and portray it broken into its hundred-or-so principal pieces:

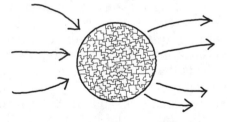

If you now go about system construction in a pure "big bang" approach (build all the pieces, integrate and test them all, deliver them all when ready), then your only metric of doneness is the final acceptance test. As a function of time, your demonstrated doneness would look like this:

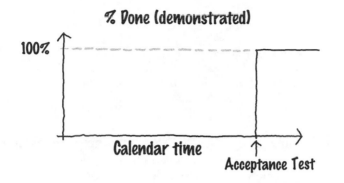

You give evidence of being 0-percent done until the very end, when you're suddenly 100-percent done. The only reason you have for believing otherwise (say, for believing at some point that you're 50-percent done) is soft evidence.

EVR is intended to give you objective evidence of partial doneness, something that will allow you to draw—and believe in—a picture like this:

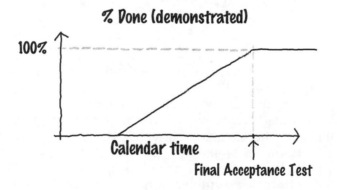

There will still be a period early in the project when progress is supported only by faith. However, from well before the project midpoint, you should be obtaining some credible EVR evidence of partial doneness.

EVR depends on your ability to build the system incrementally, say by implementing selected subsets of the system's pieces, called versions. So Version 1, for example, might be the following:

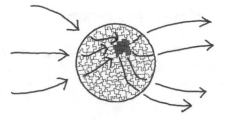

Here, you've connected (as best you can) the net inflows and out-flows to the partial product. Of course, the partial system can't do all of what the full system does, but it can do something—and that something can be tested. So you test it. You construct a Version 1 acceptance test, and when it passes, you declare that portion of the whole to be done.

Version 2 adds functionality:

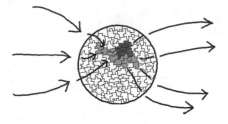

It, too, gets its own acceptance test. When it passes the test, you declare that much of the system done.

But in each case, how much is "that much"? Our brief answer is EVR, the "earned value" of the running segment. It's the portion of the whole budget that you have now "earned" credit for by demonstrating completion. (See Chapter 16 for details on computing EVR.)

If you can break up implementation into perhaps ten versions, you should be able to calculate in advance the EVR for each one and produce a table like this:

VERSION	% OF TOTAL EVR
1	11%
2	19%
3	28%
4	38%
5	51%
6	60%
7	72%
8	81%
9	94%
10	100%

Now, from the time V1 passes its version acceptance test (VAT1), you will be able to plot a curve showing the expected date of each subsequent VAT. As the tests are passed, you can track expected versus actual EVR in this form:

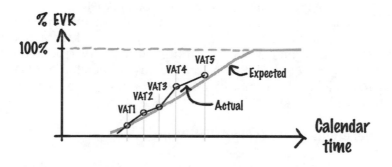

Manifestation of any of the core risks (or any major risk, for that matter) will cause marked lagging of the actual versions completed, behind the expected.

The example we've shown here is clearly concocted. But in choosing the numbers and the shape of the actual-versus-expected graph, we've tried to give you a sense of the approximate degree of control the scheme will provide.

16

INCREMENTALISM
FOR RISK MITIGATION

R isk mitigation comprises the full set of early actions you can take to make it possible later on to deal effectively (quickly, cheaply) with a risk, should it materialize.

All mitigation incurs cost and delay in the present in order to cope with possible risk manifestations later. It makes the rosy scenario somewhat less rosy, since if the risk fails to materialize, the mitigation cost might seem to have been wasted.

A bang-per-buck analysis of various risk mitigation strategies would go like this: Your *bang* is some weighted assessment of reduced cost and delay in coping with likely risk manifestations, and your *buck* is the cost and delay associated with mitigation itself. The best bang-per-buck risk mitigation strategy we know is incremental delivery.

By Incremental Delivery, We Mean . . .

Incremental delivery refers to the development of a full or nearly full design and then the implementation of that design in subsets, where each successive subset incorporates the ones that preceded it. The full strategy for incremental delivery can and should be thought out and described in an incremental delivery plan (see below) before the first increment is constructed.

The many benefits of incremental delivery have been noted often and documented by ourselves and other authors (see the

References). There are a few additional reasons why incrementalism makes particular sense to the risk manager:

- It can confirm or refute project plan hypotheses.
- It forces rank-order prioritization of system components.
- It can be used to optimize the benefit of partial deliverables (which is particularly nice if the project runs out of time and/or money).
- It provides feedback about true development efficiency.
- It positions the project for relatively painless cancellation, should that prove necessary.

As a side benefit, incremental delivery facilitates collection of the EVR metric and its objective assurance of progress.

Reactive Incrementalism (the Not-So-Great Approach)

Incremental delivery is such a win-win proposition that virtually all projects either implement the scheme or at least pay lip service to it. But sadly, the projects that could most benefit from it are often the ones that tend to adopt what we shall term a *reactive* approach to the idea.

Reactive incrementalism works like this: A project manager does some cursory hand-waving about incremental delivery but leaves the choices about subsets to the programmers. There are versions—and they are cumulative—but they're formed absent any management judgment about priorities. There is usually no published incremental delivery plan. The selection of versions is made to suit the convenience of the implementers: "Hey, these three thingamabobs all live together, so let's include them as a lump and call it Version 1." While there are versions and builds, none are ever delivered to a user. The implementers have a host of reasons for keeping the versions private—most importantly, that the versions they select tend to have no meaning to users.

All this changes when the project runs out of time. At that point, management announces that instead of delivering the whole system on the agreed date, there will be a phased delivery. The Phase One deliverable will be passed over to the new owners on the original date, but the full system will not be completed until Phase Four or Phase Nine or whatever, months or years later. This announcement is intended to allay some of the pain of lateness because the project is at least able to deliver something on the original date. But what is that something?

Because undeniable lateness tends to rear its head fairly late in the original schedule, this kind of reactive incrementalism assures that the selection of components for the initial delivery is also made late. At that point, the question, "What shall we include in the Phase One deliverable?" is somewhat bogus, since the only possible answer is, "With the delivery date so close, the Phase One deliverable has to be the stuff we've already got running."

This reactive approach has none of incrementalism's purported benefits.

Proactive Incrementalism

A proactive approach requires a very careful plan, developed well in advance, for what will be in each and every increment. Portions of the whole are selected for the early increments, based on two criteria:

- value delivered to the stakeholder
- confirmation of risk hypotheses

This forces a rank-order prioritization of system components.

Rank-ordering of all functions and features is the cure for two ugly project maladies: The first is the assumption that all parts of the product are equally important. This fiction is preserved on many projects because it assures that no one has to confront the stakeholders who have added their favorite bells and whistles as a price for their cooperation. The same fiction facilitates the second malady, *piling on,* in which features are added with the intention of overloading the project and making it fail, a favorite tactic of those who oppose the project in the first place but find it convenient to present themselves as enthusiastic project champions rather than as project adversaries.

Prioritization gives the lie to the fiction of uniform value. It facilitates an incremental cost-benefit analysis to justify early or late inclusion.

Note that value to the stakeholder is not the only basis for early inclusion. The risk-aware manager will want to force the portions involving serious technical risk into the early versions. This makes perfect sense, but it goes against the grain of most managers since it exposes their weakest hypotheses early in the game. You can understand why such managers would prefer to hold back these ticklish matters for as long as possible.

TDM: *As a novice bridge player watching one of my fraternity brothers play, I was amazed to see him lead a very weak card from his hand, which was full of high cards and trumps. I asked him about it later. He told me, "Tom, always take your losers early. Sure, I could have handily won the first six or eight tricks, but what then? With all the trumps out, if I then lose a trick, the other side gains control. I could end up sluffing off all my remaining good cards while they lead from a suit of their own choosing."*

In project work, too, it makes sense to take your losses early. When you do that, you give up control, letting events have their way with you (that's what makes it so hard). But by doing it early, you preserve your strength to come back and regain control.

Those parts of the system that depend on pulling off technical wonders should be pushed into the early versions. That way, if the wonders don't get pulled off, you maximize your options for fallback. If you do this early enough, you may be able to suffer the loss in relative private, whereas the same defeat late in the project would be immediately apparent to everyone.

Undeliverable Increments

There are projects in which actual delivery of the increments is impossible (say, a space-shot project) or not very politic. One school of thought holds that hassling with stakeholders over minor characteristics of the early versions may be so disruptive to the rest of the project that it doesn't make sense. Finally, there are projects in which you may be able to deliver some, but not all, of the increments. In any of these cases, we urge you to go about incremental implementation exactly as you would if you had planned to deliver each and every increment to the eventual user. It still makes sense to assign functions to versions based on net value to the user and technical risk. Prioritization under these circumstances means that even if your project gets canceled, you can demonstrate that no other approach would have given you as much value to put into the users' hands by the time of cancellation.

Our colleague Tom Gilb takes an extreme view of this matter: "It's as though I as a project manager weren't allowed to know the project's end date until the date arrived. The only instruction I'd get in advance would be to 'be ready to pack up whatever you've got any given morning and deliver it by close of day.' Of course that forces me to build in lots of versions (so the time between versions is relatively small) and to make sure that all the good stuff is in the early ones."[1]

The Incremental Delivery Plan

The incremental delivery plan is a formal correlation between portions of three other project artifacts:

- *the design blueprint:* a graphic showing the lowest level of modules or classes to be implemented, and their inter-relationships
- *the work breakdown structure (WBS):* the network of tasks to be completed, and their dependencies
- *the set of version acceptance tests:* the final acceptance tests for the product, broken down by version, showing which tests can be applied to which of the interim builds produced

The design blueprint is typically presented in the form of a module or class hierarchy:

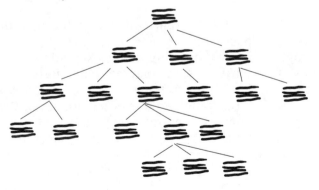

---

[1]This comment was made privately to Tom DeMarco by Tom Gilb during a meeting in Monterey, California, in 1987. You can find a more formal statement of the same ideas in Gilb's *Principles of Software Engineering Management,* ed. Susannah Finzi (Wokingham, England: Addison-Wesley, 1988).

(Here, we've concocted an abstraction of the blueprint rather than imply a preference for any particular design representation.)

Each version or increment to be produced can be portrayed as a subset of the design blueprint. Since each increment contains the ones before it, these subsets make up an onionskin partitioning of the design:

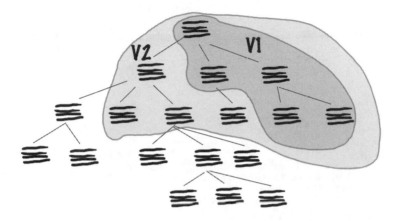

Here, Versions V1 and V2 (as well as others to come) are contained by successively larger onionskins.

Most of the tasks on the work breakdown structure can be mapped to one, and only one, version. There will always be some tasks that transcend the versions, but most will be version-specific. We associate tasks with versions based on the answer to this question:

Which tasks on the WBS are demonstrably done when Version n is done?

These are the tasks that can be mapped to Version n.

Similarly, each version maps to one and only one version acceptance test.

With this much groundwork laid, the correlation that is the heart of the incremental delivery plan can be shown in one fairly straightforward graphic:

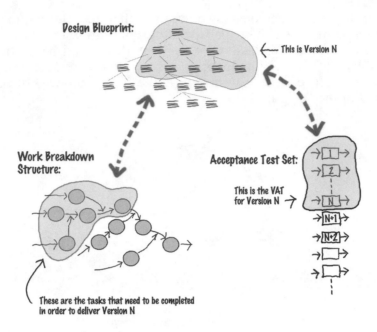

The process, in recap, follows:

- The version is identified by subsetting the design blueprint.
- The tasks associated with that version are those whose completeness is demonstrated by acceptance of the version.
- The version acceptance test for each version is the set of criteria that must be met in order to declare that version complete.

The completed incremental delivery plan can be thought of as a table with one row per version. Each row will contain, at a minimum, the following entries:

- version number
- concise statement of features and functions included, hopefully with reference to elemental requirement components contained in the specification
- pointer to version acceptance test
- expected date the version will be demonstrated complete (VAT passed)

- actual date of demonstrated completeness (to be filled in later)
- list of all tasks in the WBS proved complete by the completion of the version
- EVR of the version (discussed in the next section)

We need to place two constraints on the incremental delivery plan and its associated artifacts: First of all, the incremental approach allows for considerable time overlap among the tasks associated with the various versions, but it does not presume overlap between the task of developing the plan itself (or of the design blueprint, which precedes it) and the implementation of the versions. For this approach to work, the blueprint and incremental delivery plan must be complete before the overlapping of tasks begins.

The second constraint is that the design blueprint must show the *entirety* of the design partitioning, down to the lowest level. It's common practice to do some hand-waving at what seems to be an upper-level design, declare the design complete, and leave the rest of the design partitioning to be done as a by-product of coding. When this happens, all the advantages of the closure metrics derived from the incremental delivery plan are lost.

Calculation and Use of EVR (Pass Two)

Earned value is a measure of the projected cost of work included in a given subset of the project (it's denominated in dollars or person-days of effort). Your project is said to earn that value when that much work is done. At the beginning of the project, you have earned nothing, and at the end, you will have earned 100 percent of the budgeted amount. Of course, you may have expended more than that amount in order to earn the full budget; nonetheless, it is the budget that you are said to earn, not the actual amount of effort or money spent.

Earned value running is the cost of the work that is demonstrably complete and running in the current version. EVR is expressed as a percentage of the whole budget. The budgeted effort for each task in the WBS should similarly be expressed as a percentage of the whole. The EVR for Version n can now be calculated by adding up the contributions for all the tasks that are demonstrated complete by passing VAT n.

Consider the following simple example, a project with ten tasks in its WBS, one hundred person-weeks of scheduled effort, and an incremental delivery plan for five increments:

Task No.	Effort	Percent of Total Effort	Version with Demonstrated Completion	Subtotal	Date of Passed VAT
1.	11 person-weeks	11%	Version 1		
2.	7 person-weeks	7%	Version 1		
3.	12 person-weeks	12%	Version 1	30%	Day-100
4.	10 person-weeks	10%	Version 2		
5.	9 person-weeks	9%	Version 2	49%	Day-154
6.	8 person-weeks	8%	Version 3		
7.	13 person-weeks	13%	Version 3	69%	Day-173
8.	9 person-weeks	9%	Version 4	78%	Day-185
9.	14 person-weeks	14%	Version 5		
10.	7 person-weeks	7%	Version 5	100%	Day-206

The full project is complete when Version 5 has passed its acceptance test, VAT5 (since V5 is the final version, VAT5 is the full product acceptance test). At that point, 100 percent of the value is said to be earned and running. The EVR associated with passing each of the VATs is

VAT1: 30%
VAT2: 49%
VAT3: 69%
VAT4: 78%
VAT5: 100%

The graph of actual EVR demonstrated as a function of time looks like this:

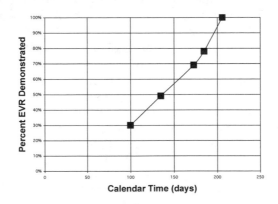

The amount of EVR demonstrated complete per unit of time establishes a glide path for the project. This glide path is the strongest possible indicator of the approach to project completion. Deviations of the glide path from the expected path are a sure sign of risk manifestation, and they serve as a call to action to put into place planned risk containment strategies.

Incrementalism: A Summing Up

The incremental approach to product development is a major source of closure metrics, and closure metrics are the pulse of the project. By monitoring EVR and tracking actual production rate in terms of EVR, you are using a "voice of the product" metric. The product itself is telling you, "I am such-and-such percent done, and I can prove it." The proof, of course, is the passing of a version acceptance test on an increment that includes that percentage of the full project's earned value.

EVR tracking is the principal source of feedback about risk from the project midpoint (or even slightly earlier) all the way to completion. EVR provides a voice-of-the-product metric while imposing only small additional cost on the project.

So far, we've called out only the risk-related benefits of an incremental approach. For the record, there are other benefits as well, including

1. more closure to keep project staff motivated
2. more visibility
3. more user involvement in the project, from midpoint to end
4. possibility of eliminating the tail end of the project upon realizing that it mostly consists of bells and whistles (the low-benefit portions of the product)

Incrementalism is a good idea for all projects . . . and a must when risks are high.

17

THE ULTIMATE
RISK MITIGATION STRATEGY

Indulge us for a moment, here, for a brief thought experiment. This is going to be good. Imagine you find yourself working at a client site in Chicago. It's a Wednesday afternoon. You learn there's a very important meeting scheduled for noon on Friday, in San Francisco. The politics of the situation dictate that you *must* be there, and the complex personalities of some of the people involved suggest that it would be a disaster to be late. You just simply have to be there on time.

You hop onto the Web and discover that American Airlines has an 8:40 A.M. departure from O'Hare with space available, and planned arrival time in SFO at 11:21 A.M. Let's see, hand baggage only, probably no line for cabs at that hour, and the traffic on 101 North is likely to be . . . not too terrible. If you catch a break here and there on flight departures, no gate holds, no backup over San Francisco, no noontime traffic snarl, you're probably going to be at the San Francisco office with five to ten minutes to spare.

But now hold on, a plan that depends on "catching a break here and there" is hardly risk-free. If you don't catch all of those breaks, you'll be late. No good. So, now you go into risk-mitigation mode. How should you alter your plan to protect yourself from the evident risks?

This is a no-brainer. We don't have to be mind readers to guess that your very first impulse is to consider *starting earlier.* That crack-of-dawn flight leaving at 6 A.M. would be a chore to make, but it would give you a few hours of slack on the other end. Or, how about leaving the night before and putting up at a hotel near the office?

Your "project" in this case is getting to San Francisco. The more important it is that you finish that project on time, the more inclined you are to start it early. That's probably obvious to everyone . . . aside from IT people, that is.

The Joke's On Us

We could make a little joke about how we IT people approach risk containment compared to everyone else. That joke would go something like this:

> An IT manager and a normal person are both working in Chicago on a Wednesday afternoon when they learn that they have to be in San Francisco for a noon meeting on Friday and that it's imperative to be on time. The normal person—let's call her Diane—takes a Thursday evening flight and checks herself into that pleasant little hotel just down the block from the San Francisco office. She has a leisurely dinner at Hunam and wanders over to Union Street to take in a film. The next morning, she has a relaxed breakfast and works on her laptop until eleven. She checks out at 11:30 and strolls into the office ten minutes early.
>
> Meanwhile, the IT manager, Jack, has booked himself on the 8:40, Friday morning. He catches a cab midtown at 7:05 and runs into a traffic jam on the Eisenhower. He complains angrily to the cabdriver all the way out to O'Hare. The stupid driver just can't be made to understand that it is essential that Jack make this flight. When he checks in at United, he tells the check-in clerk rather forcefully that the flight must take off and land on time, no excuses. He tells her that he will be "very, very disappointed" with any lateness. When a gate hold is announced, Jack jumps up and objects loudly. When a revised departure time is announced, he digs deep into his bag of managerial tools and delivers the ultimate pronouncement: "If you people don't get me into San Francisco in time for my noon meeting, HEADS WILL ROLL!"

For a project with a critical delivery date, starting early is real risk-mitigation. It's probably the only effective way to contain the risk of lateness for most projects. Yes, we know, it's already too late to start your project early; it started when it started, and now you're in the soup. And you're not reading this book to learn how you might have avoided getting in the soup in the first place. You want to work your way out of it. That's all true. But the early-start option is valuable to you anyway, as you'll see below.

Gutsy and Gutless Management

First, we need to take on a bit of organizational folklore that will otherwise get in the way—the notion that initiating a project without slack is the sign of really gutsy management. On the contrary, it is a sign of cowardice.

To see this, we need to consider the circumstances surrounding a typical project kickoff decision. They might go something like this:

> The economy is currently in a downspin, but it should turn around within the next two quarters. Starting now to build our new product version would give us a head start on the competition when the market comes to life again—so we should get started forthwith on the project. Only, what if the market doesn't turn when we expect it to? Maybe we'd better wait to see what actually happens. If demand picks up early next year, we can start the project then. And if it's sleepy until summer, we'll be able to coast along without project expense until then.

This is gutless management at its worst.

The gutsy manager, on the other hand, is willing to take on a bit of risk to emerge with an enhanced position if risk-taking pays off. Starting projects early enough always takes guts. It always requires someone to make a case that the market has not yet already made. It involves putting down chips on something that is not a perfectly sure bet.

It's ironic that so many projects find themselves running the risk of late delivery because managers have walked away from that other, much more important risk—making an early start.

Why the Early Start Option Is Important Even If You Can't Do It

Projects that finish late are almost always projects that started far too late. And projects that start too late are a sign of missing vision and courage at the top of the managerial ladder. When you're under the gun and being chided for not finishing soon enough, you need to be quick to note that the project was not started early enough. This is a mantra that most organizations would do well to adopt.

TDM: *Early in 1996, one of my clients was the manager of a large embedded-system software project. Her job was to produce the control software for a new line of products that marketing was extremely eager to launch. The major stakeholder was a marketing manager named Hans, who had proposed the project and gotten it funded. Hans was angry when my client's team came up with a 4Q97 schedule. He had been hoping for March 31, 1997. He denounced her estimate at a public meeting as not aggressive enough, and he followed up (unfortunately for him) with the statement: "I can prove to you that beyond March, every month that this product is not ready to ship will cost this company one-hundred-ten-thousand dollars in lost profit."*

I queried him on his assertion. "Hans, would that same figure apply to delivery before March thirty-first, as well? If we delivered by the end of February, for example, would that give us an additional hundred-ten-thousand dollars of profit, beyond the revenue stream that you have projected?"

"Yes," he said. "Definitely."

"And an end-of-January delivery?" I pressed on. "Would that make us yet another one-hundred-ten-thousand-dollar profit?"

"Yes," he said.

"If we could put the product in your hands today"—that was February 1996, when the project had just been funded—"would you be collecting that additional hundred-ten-thousand dollars per month for the rest of the year?"

"Yes," he said, a bit less sure of himself now.

"Well then, Hans, you obviously started this project much too late. If you'd kicked it off eighteen months ago, we could be shipping now, and all those months of hundred-ten-thousand-dollars' extra profit . . ." I let him figure out the implications.

PART IV

HOW MUCH

- How much risk can we afford to take?
- How does value offset risk?
- How can we realistically expect to assess the value (benefit) of a new project?
- How can we be certain that the value expected is actually received?
- How do we deal with value that is itself uncertain?
- What sense is there to a cost-benefit justification that attempts to compare an uncertain cost to an uncertain benefit?

18

VALUE QUANTIFICATION

In the beginning—the early days of the IT industry—the justifi-cation of new systems products was pretty straightforward. The systems we were installing then were usually replacements for manual clerical schemes. The labor saved was the value, and the development expense was the cost. The cost-benefit study came up with nice formulations like this:

$$\text{Return on Investment} = \frac{\text{Value} - \text{Cost}}{\text{Cost}}$$

To show we had a hardheaded respect for the time value of money, we expressed the various streams of costs and savings in terms of net present value (NPV). We could make easy state-ments of the form, "deciding to kick this project off now is the equivalent of adding a net present value of $1.3 million into the corporate coffers today."

Sometimes, the justifications took slightly different forms:

TDM: One of my early management responsibilities was to run
         a project that installed a centralized billing application in
         the French National Merchandise Mart at La Villette, in
         Paris. The new Mart was planned to replace the old
         one at Les Halles. At La Villette, all billing information
         was transmitted digitally. The manual form of the same

function at Les Halles had utilized a network of pneumatic tubes to send chits and receipts and invoices whizzing around the floor under air pressure. The pneumatic tube network had been installed at Les Halles in time for the World Exposition of 1897. In 1897, there wasn't much in the way of rubber products to make an airtight seal, so the tubes were all made of lead. When they built Les Halles, the price of lead was only a few centimes per kilogram. When we tore it down, the price of lead was more than seven francs per kilogram. And there was a lot of lead. The salvage value of the lead was enough to pay for the entire project, including all the hardware and software.

What's Different Today?

Times have changed. Most of the direct cost-saving systems were built long ago. Today, instead of building systems that offset cost, we more often embark on projects intended to improve our position in a market. These market-enhancing systems are much more complicated to justify. We as an industry have fallen into the habit of a less rigorous justification. New systems are often justified with statements like, "We gotta have it," or, "This system is necessary for us to remain competitive."

While the benefit side of the cost-benefit analysis was becoming ever softer, requirements for rigor and precision on the cost side were increasing. So, it became common to see a new project justification like this:

$$Cost = \$6,235,812.55$$
$$Benefit = \text{"We gotta have it."}$$

When projects have precisely limited costs and only vaguely stated benefits, development personnel are held accountable for costs and nobody is held accountable for benefit realization. The project is then inclined to shed functionality willy-nilly in order to meet cost targets. Since nobody bothered to state where the greatest benefits lay, there is no valid basis for shedding one function as opposed to another. The most common result is poor benefit realization and pointing fingers on all sides.

Precisely stated costs and vaguely hinted-at benefits make a travesty of cost-benefit analysis. More importantly, they also make sensible risk management impossible. When risks are considered in isolation, there is no way to justify any given amount of risk. The result is that only the most risk-averse approach seems to make sense.

This is all leading toward an inevitable principle:

> Costs and benefits need to be specified with equal precision.

When benefit cannot be stated more precisely than "We gotta have it," then the cost specification should be "It's gonna be expensive." If the costs are specified with a clearly implemented risk diagram, the benefits have to be stated in a similar form (for more about this, see Chapters 21 to 23).

The Question of Accountability

When development managers are held accountable, they are obliged to come up with explicitly stated time and cost budgets, annotated for intrinsic uncertainty (in the form of a risk diagram, for example). Then, they must manage their projects to conform to their predictions. The two components here are performance-predicted and performance-realized.

Similarly, the stakeholders have to be held accountable for benefit-predicted and benefit-realized. The precision or imprecision of these benefit quantifications has to be more or less equivalent to the precision or imprecision of the costs.

Remedial Moment: The 45,328 Reasons We Can't Specify Benefits Precisely

Rationalization for poorly projected benefits has become astonishingly adept. The most typical variant is of the form, "The benefit of this system is that we get to <expletive> survive." As our colleague Mike Silves points out, this is a pure power play. Survival can be expressed in terms of market penetration, top-line revenue, earnings, repeat business, and the like, all of which are quantifiable. The power play asserts that the requester should be excused from menial considerations like quantification because of the importance of the request, not to mention the importance of the requester. More essential, though, is the hidden need of the requester not to be made accountable in any way for how the system he or she is proposing actually translates into financial reward.

Other reasons companies don't do careful benefit predictions and benefit-realization assessments include the following:

- The system is too small for us to bother.
- There is no choice about whether or not to build this system.
- The system is required by a regulatory authority.
- The benefit depends entirely on meeting the market window.
- The system is a replacement for an existing system.
- The request comes down from on high.
- The benefit is too uncertain to quantify precisely.
- The stakeholder has said, "Trust me, it's worth doing."
- The benefit numbers wouldn't be credible anyway.

On this last point, our colleague Steve McMenamin, at the time a vice president of Edison International, offered this observation:

> There is a class of purported savings that I term "general productivity." These are of the form: "If we implement the new data-mining system, each employee will save at least two minutes per day, which adds up to annual savings across our whole organization of forty-two kajillion dollars." It's not that there isn't a grain of potential truth in such claims. But they're such a reliable hiding place for stupid projects and the consultants who propose them that claims of "general productivity" benefits receive withering and usually well-deserved scorn. I typically discount them by at least one-hundred percent.

The gripe here is about having tiny benefits distributed widely. When productivity benefits are huge and concentrated, the justification can be much more compelling.

Not included in our list of reasons companies don't do careful benefit predictions and benefit-realization assessments is one that is often applicable but never mentioned: The benefits are minuscule or nonexistent. As a general rule of thumb, when benefits are not quantified at all, assume there aren't any.

Your Company's Biggest Risks

What has any of this got to do with risk and risk management? Our treatment of risk management so far has been targeted at the project- or IT-manager level. Now raise your perspective a level or two higher. While IT's biggest risks are either technological (product-related) or sociological (project-related), the *company's* biggest risks are value-related: wasted effort on low-value projects, and the opportunity cost of missing high-value projects.

An aggressive risk-taking posture has to be steered by benefit. How much risk you're willing to take has to be a function of how much benefit there is to capture.

TRL: *In the 1990's, many of my clients got fixated on improving the wrong process. They were all hung up on the how-projects-are-built process. The one that really matters is the process that determines which projects are worth doing. Ironically, in some of the most process-aware companies I know, there is no defined process for project initiation—it's all done by fiat.*

Five Elements of Benefit Calculation

Insisting that accountability for system value be equivalent to accountability for costs leads to the following benefit-calculation scheme:

- Stakeholders declare expected benefits at the same time that developers declare expected costs and schedules, and to equivalent precision.
- Stakeholders express the uncertainty in their benefit expectation in the same way that developers indicate the uncertainty in their cost and schedule calculations (see Chapter 21 for details).
- Stakeholders assess the relative value of system components in order to provide a basis for version selection and to perform sensible sensitivity analysis and incremental cost-benefit analysis (details in Chapter 22).
- Management justifies the project based on a careful comparison of benefits and costs and their attendant uncertainties (details in Chapter 23).
- Management assesses benefit-realized after the fact and provides the assessment as input into the postmortem process.

This approach is broadly what Barry Boehm calls Value-Based Software Engineering. Boehm comments on the need for value-basing:

> *Software engineering is fundamentally a contact sport. In software engineering as in rugby, no amount of theory about how to succeed in a scrum is going to come close to real experience in the middle of a few scrums.*
>
> *Further, the theory that most current students get covers maybe 15% of the activities they encounter in practice. Most of it is based on a model of software engineering as a set-piece job of deriving and verifying code from a static set of requirements. This was a good model in the 1970's . . . but it's way out of date now. In the 1970's, software was a small part of most systems, and the stability of the requirements meant that you could often "separate concerns" and just attack the problem of deriving code from software requirements in isolation. But all of that has changed now. Software is critically bound to a system's value-added, its flexibility is the key to adaptation to change, and software engineering is less and less "all about programming."*[1]

In this view, the focus is as much on the value to be realized as on the "set piece" of software production.

---

[1] Barry W. Boehm, "Software Engineering Is a Value-Based Contact Sport," *IEEE Software* (Sept.–Oct. 2002), pp. 95–97. Reprinted by permission.

19

VALUE IS UNCERTAIN, TOO

Stakeholders often excuse themselves from predicting new-system value because they reason that it's too uncertain to predict. The truest answer they can think of when queried about expected value is, "I don't know." Stakeholders need to have the same knee-jerk reaction we urged upon you in Chapter 11: When they hear themselves saying "I don't know," they need to switch gears into uncertainty-bounding mode and begin drawing uncertainty diagrams.

Benefit? Well, That Depends ...

For systems whose major effect is market enhancement rather than cost displacement, there are some real unknowns about likely benefit. The market may leap all over a new product, or it may respond with a *ho hum*. The competition may steal a march on the new product, either coming out earlier with a similar product or announcing a forthcoming set of enticing and differentiating features.

Whatever happens may reduce the actual value of the new system from its most optimistic expectation. The very formulation of such a doubt calls attention to the fact that there is a "most optimistic expectation." The first step in value prediction is to quantify the most optimistic expectation and to express it in terms of dollars of revenue or earnings, or added points of market penetration. Similarly, the least optimistic expectation can be quantified. Someplace in between the two is the most likely expectation. These three points produce a rudimentary uncertainty diagram, bounding the risks associated with value to be received:

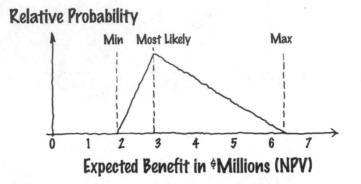

People persuaded to commit themselves to this extent will insist on attaching some explicit *stakeholder assumptions* to the expectation, a variation on the project manager's project assumptions—the risks that he or she is not managing and are therefore someone else's responsibility. A stakeholder assumption might be something like, "All bets are off if the system turns out to be unstable."

For every incremental uncertainty diagram, such as the one presented above, there is an equivalent in cumulative form, such as this:

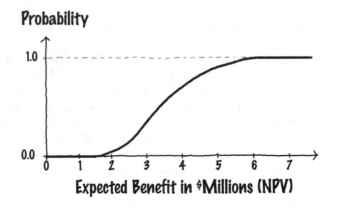

From this, we can derive all kinds of useful information, including mean expected benefit and the expected benefit for any required confidence level. We can even use Monte Carlo tools to simulate the project multiple times and to produce a graph showing the benefit received for each instance.

The Market Window

The grand illusion of a market window is probably the safest and most often utilized excuse for not doing careful benefit projections. A stakeholder may speak confidently about benefits that will only be possible if the developers have the system ready before the market window closes. Any benefit number will do here because the allied tactic is to assert that the market window will close by a date that is virtually impossible to meet. The project is thus set up to fail, but the stakeholder avoids all accountability.

Market windows in the future are easy enough to talk about, but there are damn few examples you can dredge up from the past. VisiCalc clearly got its product to market before any market window had closed, but how to explain Lotus Notes? And all supposed market windows for spreadsheets had long since closed before Excel came along. How confusing, then, that Excel became the dominant spreadsheet. And Google, which missed its market window by a country mile, could obviously never become the dominant search engine—only somehow it did.

If the market window has any significance at all, it certainly isn't binary. The pushback to the stakeholders is to oblige them to commit themselves to the benefits expected for the entire range of possible delivery dates. The range of dates covered by the development team's risk diagram should also be covered by the stakeholders' set of diagrams showing benefit expected for delivery at dates across the range. It's not so easy to game the diagram set. Showing zero or negative value from a delivery that's later than a given date may come back to bite the person who asserts the dire outcome. Since value is at the heart of the larger risk facing an organization, playing fast and loose with value projections (either under- or over-assessing them) will not be viewed as a mark of honor.

News from the Real World

To complement our own experience in value assessment, we queried a small set of real-world managers who have made it work (and have sometimes come a cropper). As you'll see, there is a fascinating mixture of success and failure:

> "The larger the system, the more accountability . . . the [benefit] numbers are watched carefully, because future financial models for overhead will be reduced due to the promises. . . .
>
> "There is always the situation where the right person makes the request. Every organization has a few individuals who can simply get what they want due to their importance to the company."
> —*Christine Davis, formerly of TI and Raytheon*

> "[proceeding without value assessment] leaves nothing but testosterone-based decision making. It's been my experience that testosterone-based decision making doesn't have a very good track record at producing value over the long term. In fact, I think that it's a career-limiting approach at best. . . .
>
> "I've also experienced a very weird approach to accountability that goes something like, 'The project was a complete success (after we redefined "success," that is).' This usually follows one of those late-project 'flight from functionality' sessions. Seems like a fuzz sandwich: fuzz at the front of the project, and fuzz at the end of the project with some sort of meat (you hope, but you don't look to closely) in the middle."
> —*Sean Jackson, Howard Hughes Medical Institute*

> "[there has to be an] equality of accountability between builders and stakeholders. The stakeholder is accountable to make sure value is produced. [But] we find pretty consistently in our surveys that companies don't track after the fact whether or not benefits are realized."
> —*Rob Austin, Professor, Harvard Business School*

> "The savings figures also are classified by whether they are reductions or avoided costs. The difference is important. Reductions are decrements from current approved budget levels. You (the requesting manager) already have the money; you are agreeing to give it up if you get the money for the new system. Avoided cost savings are of this form: 'If

I don't have this system, I will have to hire another <n>
<worker-type> in <future-year>. But if I do get the system, I
can avoid this cost.' This is every system requester's favorite
kind of benefit: all promise, no pain. The catch is that there
is no reason to believe you'd ever have been funded to hire
those additional workers. You're trading off operating funds
you may never get in the future for capital funds today. Very
tempting, but most request-evaluators see this coming from
miles away. The correct test for avoided-cost benefits is
whether the putative avoidable cost is otherwise unavoid-
able, in other words, that the future budget request would
inevitably be approved. This is a tough test, but real
avoided-cost benefits can and do pass it."

—*Steve McMenamin, Atlantic Systems Guild*

The picture that emerged from our informal interviews was in
some ways its own kind of fuzz sandwich, but there were a couple
of interesting trends:

1. Best-practice organizations are intent on doing value
   assessment, though they may be willing to vary its form
   from project to project.
2. Lots of them follow the scheme of reducing downstream
   budgets by the amount of the expected benefit, what
   Christine referred to in saying, "future financial models
   for overhead will be reduced due to the promises."

Finally, even these organizations have some instances of value
guaranteed by promises like "Trust me, there is benefit to doing
this," but this is usually limited to stakeholders who have accountability for both cost and benefit.

20

SENSITIVITY ANALYSIS

The delicate matter at the heart of this chapter is increased stakeholder accountability. We've already proposed the necessity of thrusting responsibility for value projection and measurement of realized value onto a system's users and stakeholders (to the same precision as cost estimates and actuals). Now we would have you make the case for some incrementalism in this value accounting. This is delicate because you can't simply *oblige* your clients to be that accountable. You have to wheedle and persuade and call in favors. Do you really want to spend whatever political capital you may have on these seemingly abstruse matters? In this chapter, we are going to try to persuade you that you do.

If This Is the Solution, What Is the Problem?

The problem we take aim at here is the package-deal nature of most system projects. A project gets funding based on some value—either expressly quantified or not—that the resulting product will deliver. Now it's worth asking several questions: Where is that value in the product? Is it uniformly distributed around all the system's components? Is there an equal proportion of value in this 100-line edit as in that 100-line module over there that reconfigures after a power failure?

Don't bet on it. Our experience (and yours, admit it) suggests that value is very unevenly distributed over a system. The system's real money proposition lies in certain core functions performed at or near the product's heart.

Sometimes, this heart-of-the-value region constitutes no more than 10 percent of the code. The rest is . . . well, what is it? Sometimes, it's necessary infrastructural support; other times, it's pure bells and whistles, masquerading as necessary infrastructure. Cutting through this little deception is what sensitivity analysis is all about.

Incremental Value/Cost Analysis

Once we divide a system up into pieces (say, the functions at spec time or the modules at design time), it's possible and sensible to allocate projected cost on the map of that partitioning. So, a portion of the system costed out at about $235,000 might have a cost map that looks like this:

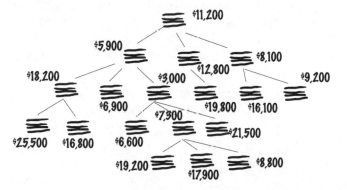

Now, if the stakeholders could be persuaded to distribute over the same map their assessment of the value that the system is expected to deliver, we would have both a cost and a value figure for each component. We could compute a value/cost ratio for each piece.

We know, we know—you're never going to be able to pull this off. But just imagine that you could. What would you do with the incremental value/cost figures? That's an easy one. You'd use them to separate core functionality from necessary infrastructure from bells and whistles. You'd do this without ever having to pronounce loaded words like "bells and whistles." The stakeholders' own value assessments would give the lie to the presumption of value uniformity across the whole system.

Some of the components would have high value/cost ratios, and those would be candidates for early delivery. You'd formulate your version plan to pick up the highest-ratio components in early versions. With Version n delivered, all or most participants may discover that the average value/cost ratio of the not-yet-implemented portions was poor. This might well cause a groundswell of consensus to end the project, call it a grand success, and go on to other things. All without you ever having to take the unpopular position that so-and-so's favorite function was a pure sop to his ego and had damn little contribution to the overall value proposition.

Economies and Diseconomies of Scale

The news that value is not uniform over a system suggests a useful tactical tool for the IT manager. System projects are known to exhibit diseconomy-of-scale characteristics: Doubling the size of a system should be expected to more than double the effort required to build it. This nonlinearity of effort with respect to system size has been well documented by Boehm and others:

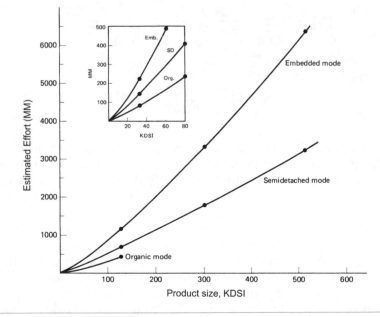

---

[1]Barry W. Boehm, *Software Engineering Economics* (Englewood Cliffs, N.J.: Prentice-Hall, 1981), p. 76. Reprinted by permission of Pearson Education, Inc., Upper Saddle River, N.J.

If increasing the size of a product exposes you to more-than-proportional increases in cost, then decreasing product size offers the possibility of more-than-proportional savings. Eliminating those portions of the system where the value/cost ratio is low is probably the easiest and best way to relax constraints on time and budget. It's odd that software builders should come to believe that "build less software" ought to be part of their mantra, but the advantages are apparent.

Back to the Real World

Okay, let's face facts: Getting your stakeholders to do incremental value projections is going to be like pulling teeth. It's a nontrivial amount of work, it opens the door for an additional level of accountability, and it has no obvious payback for the people sticking their necks out and doing the quantification. If there are bells and whistles lurking among the useful functions, the very people who have to do the quantification may be the ones likely to lose favorite features. You can expect almost any stakeholder to object strenuously to the effort and to assure you in the most earnest tones that "It's *all* necessary to support core functionality. Honest." This is the same tired, old value-is-equally-distributed line, but don't expect to convince them of that.

Maybe you don't have to. The payoff of incremental value/cost data is that it allows you to rank-order components for inclusion in the versions. The actual ratios would be nice, but if you couldn't have them, wouldn't you settle for the rank-ordering, instead?

The very fact that you will be implementing incrementally gives you a lever for extracting rank-ordering instructions from even the most unwilling stakeholders. After all, some parts of the system will necessarily have to be implemented after some others. Some pieces will be first and some will be last. If you throw that back in your stakeholders' laps, they will leap to tell you about order of implementation. Everybody knows that sometimes systems come in late and that portions implemented early are likely to be available by the original date while late-implemented portions are not. It would be a rare user who failed to take advantage of this additional level of control, even though availing himself or herself of it would be an effective admission of uneven concentration of value in various portions of the system.

21

VALUE OFFSETS RISK

How much risk should we be willing to take on a given project? Whatever answer you come up with has to account for the potential value the project could deliver. No workable philosophy of risk-taking can ignore value. When the stakes are high, it's worth running even serious risks. When the stakes are low, almost no risk should be tolerable.

If that paragraph seemed reasonable to you, you are in the minority. The IT industry seems to subscribe to an almost opposite philosophy: *Take lots of risks when the benefit is negligible. How else can we possibly get costs down enough to justify this loser of a project?*

This thinking has been the genesis of one of the most common but infamous working styles in our industry. . . .

Death-March Projects

On a death march, unflinching sacrifice from each and every project member is absolutely required. The project demands abandonment of personal life, tons of overtime, Saturdays and Sundays in the office, estrangement from family, and so on. Nothing less than total dedication to the project can be accepted.

Justification for the death march always takes the form of project importance: *This effort is so essential that it requires the utmost of project personnel.* But there is a bit of a conundrum built into that statement. If the project is so essential, why can't the company spend the time and money required to do it properly?

In our experience, the one common characteristic among death-march projects is low expected value. They are projects aimed at putting out products of monumental insignificance. The only real justification for the death march is that with value so minuscule, doing the project at normal cost would clearly result in costs that are greater than benefits. Only with heroic effort can one hope to make the pig fly.

A second characteristic of death-march projects is that people are gulled into robbing their personal lives for the company's benefit, believing that doing so will alone be sufficient to bring home a minuscule-value endeavor at so low a price that it all makes sense.

The third characteristic of death-march projects is that they almost always end up as total fiascoes with little or nothing delivered (usually at above-average cost) and with everyone feeling stupid and angry. There has to be a better way.

Take Risks Justified by Value

The better way is to let expected value guide you in deciding how much risk to run. In retrospect, the main reason we haven't done this before is that we lacked the discipline to force value quantification. Particularly on low-value projects, we stood by a firm refusal to quantify value—it was the only way to keep the whole matter looking respectable. In the absence of declared value expectations, it was possible to make the case based on reduced development cost alone. The justification was essentially, "We'll get the costs down so low that they'll certainly be less than whatever value is reaped."

Real project justification (you always knew this in your heart) requires balancing risk against value, as shown in this figure:

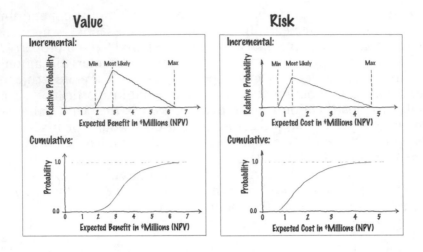

There is a mechanical problem here: how to decide whether the value shown on the left side does indeed offset the risk on the right. Since both value and risk are uncertain, to some degree, you would expect the trade-off to have some uncertainty about it, too. Recourse to hairy mathematics would provide us with an uncertainty diagram showing the combined effect of uncertain value versus uncertain risk. However, without using calculus, the best we can do is a RISKOLOGY simulation that shows the net benefit for a series of one hundred simulated projects. It produces a bar graph approaching the smooth figure shown here:

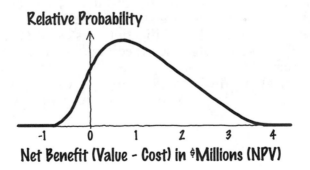

This simulation suggests that about one project in ten will have costs that exceed the value received. Nine times out of ten, though, the project should be expected to have at least some net benefit, with a net present value of $1.5 million, representing the approximate fifty-fifty expectation. Putting a few million dollars at risk for a fifty-fifty expectation of $1.5 million in net gains is a pretty respectable undertaking. Of course, if there is another project with a better net benefit profile, you'll want to do that one instead. You have only a limited amount of risk capital to play with; the net benefit uncertainty diagrams guide you in deciding where to put it.

22

REFINING THE
RISK MANAGEMENT
PRESCRIPTION

To finish up, we return to the prescription first laid out in Chapter 10, to add a few refinements. Here we build on that chapter's first section: "What It Means to Do Risk Management."

What It Means to Do Risk Management (Refined and Elaborated)

Risk management is essentially the performance—integrated into the project—of the following steps (Items 6 through 12 have the most refinements versus the list from Chapter 10, but be sure to review the full process):

1. Use a risk-discovery process (Chapter 14) to compile a census of the risks facing your project.
2. Make sure all the core risks of software projects (Chapter 13) are represented in your census.
3. Do all the following homework on a per-risk basis:

   - Give the risk a name and unique number.
   - Brainstorm to find a transition indicator—the earliest practical indication of materialization—for the risk.
   - Estimate the cost and schedule impact if the risk should materialize.

- Estimate the probability of risk materialization.
- Calculate the schedule and budget exposure for the risk.
- Determine in advance what contingency actions the project will need to take if and when transition occurs.
- Determine what mitigation actions need to be taken in advance of transition, to make the selected contingency actions feasible.
- Add mitigation actions to the overall project plan.
- Write all the details down on a template like the one in Appendix B.

4. Designate showstoppers as project assumptions. Perform the ritual of passing each of these risks upward.

5. Make a first pass at schedule estimation by assuming that *no risks will materialize.* In other words, your initial estimating step is to determine the nano-percent date (see Chapter 10), the earliest date by which you can't prove to yourself that you won't be done. This is different from established industry practice in that we suggest you use the nano-percent date as an *input* to the scheduling process, not as an output of it. Derive N using a parametric estimation tool, if you have one, tuned to its most optimistic settings.

6. Download RISKOLOGY (see http://www.systems guild.com/riskology). Enter your project parameters on the main worksheet. While you're at it, enter all the customization factors you can find, based on supporting data from your company records. Override as much of the simulator's industry data about core risks as you can, substituting credible data from your own environment. Add customized worksheets for all the non-core risks you're tracking. Run the simulation to produce a risk diagram for your project, forcing the intersection to your nano-percent date.

7. Express all commitments from this point forward using risk diagrams, explicitly showing the uncertainty associated with each projected date and budget. Rather than explain the concept of a risk diagram to any of your less-than-savvy stakeholders, refer to it as a simulation of your project, run five hundred times,

showing all the possible outcomes and the relative likelihood of each.

8. Create a work breakdown structure showing all the tasks needed to complete the project. Estimate the effort required for each task, using whatever scheme you currently employ. We're going to be using these estimates in a slightly less-than-conventional way: Only the relative weights of the task efforts will matter, not the absolute values. These relative weights will be required input to the calculation of the EVR metrics.

9. At the start of the project, force commitment on net dataflows in and out of the product. You should be able to come up with a complete definition of all net input and output flows—down to the data element level—within the first 12 to 15 percent of calendar time. Treat sign-off on these net flows as a major project milestone. Don't proceed to later tasks if this milestone hasn't been passed. Remember, failure of this closure metric, the net flows sign-off, is a potential fatal warning.

10. Force a complete design partitioning prior to any implementation. Use this as input to the process of creating an incremental delivery plan.

11. When the design partitioning is complete, revisit the work breakdown structure, reestimate task weights, and express tasks as percentages of the remaining work to be done.

12. Assess value to the same precision as cost.

13. Break the requirements contained in the specification down to their elemental level. Number them in a rank-order by priority. Use net value to the user and technical risk as the two criteria for prioritization.

14. Create an incremental delivery plan in which the whole product is broken into versions (lots of versions, at least enough to schedule a new version every week or so). Assign all the elemental requirements to their versions, with the higher-priority items coming earlier. Calculate EVR for each version and record it in the plan. Treat the incremental delivery plan as a major project deliverable.

15. Create an overall final product-acceptance test, divided into VATs, one per version.
16. Plot out EVR versus the expected delivery date of each version. As the versions pass their VATs, place the actual results on the same graph.
17. Throughout the rest of the project, monitor all risks for transition and/or expiration, and execute contingency plans whenever materialization occurs. Monitor the EVR glide path and its performance against the expected path. Treat deviations as a sign of possible risk manifestation.
18. Keep the risk-discovery process going throughout the project to cope with late-appearing risks.

PART V

WHETHER OR NOT

- How do we know whether or not risk management is really being practiced?

23

TEST FOR
RISK MANAGEMENT

Whether you are the one responsible for risk management or
you are somewhere above that responsibility in the hierarchy, you need some objective way to understand whether or not
the work is being done. But why is that? Why can't you just
assume that people responsible for managing projects will be naturally drawn to managing project risks? The reason is that there
are powerful false-positive indicators at work in organizations.
These false-positives tend to give an unwarranted pass to anything
that calls itself management.

Imagine that you are managing above the project level and
that risk management should be taking place at the project level
(within the projects or peer to them). The false-positive indicator
works like this: You reason, "Hey, my people are running risky
endeavors, so of course they are managing the risks. What is
management, after all, but anticipating and steering around the
various obstacles that might sink the project? My managers are
professionals—they certainly wouldn't let themselves focus only
on the easy stuff and ignore the real dangers."

Sounds good. The only problem is that this line of thinking
ignores all the disincentives built into or buried in the *corporate
culture*. These include can-do thinking, an unwillingness to dis-
appoint, the imperative to preserve the rosiness of the rosy scenario, the fear of expressing uncertainty, the need to appear in
control (even when real control is illusive), the temptation to use

political power to trump reality, and the kind of short-term thinking that plagues all human endeavors.

These are powerful forces. They can make apparently thoughtful people shy away from reasonable management and adopt instead *reasonable-seeming* management. There is a difference.

A set of objective tests to determine whether or not risk management is actually taking place can be of value not only to upper management, but also to risk managers themselves.

The *Did We Really Do Risk Management?* Test

When risk management is happening and becoming established in the corporate culture, projects will pass all or most of the following tests:

1. There is a census of risks. The risks in the census include all the core risks of software projects plus the risks that are unique to that project. The risks are causal in nature (things that will cause the dreaded outcomes rather than just the dreaded outcomes themselves).

2. There is an ongoing risk-discovery process in place. Risk discovery is open and welcoming to all participants. Specific steps are taken to make it safe during risk discovery to articulate unwelcome ideas. There may even be an anonymous channel open for people to convey bad news. This is a scheme that works well in some of our client companies. (It's not used often, but when it is, it's *invaluable*.)

3. There are uncertainty diagrams everywhere. They are used to quantify the causal risks and to convey aggregate risks and expectations. The corporate culture is beginning to think it unprofessional to make commitments without explicitly noted uncertainty.

4. There are both goals and estimates for the project, and they are never the same. Goals may be at or near the nano-percent performance level, but the estimates must be much more conservative. If the goal is a twelve-month delivery for a given project, the estimate should project that delivery will occur at least as far out as Month 18. In any event, the specific confidence level to

be associated with any commitment is indicated by the uncertainty diagram.

5. Each risk has a designated transition indicator. There is ongoing transition monitoring to detect risk materialization.

6. Each risk has an associated contingency plan and a mitigation plan. Contingent actions are included in the work breakdown structure as possible activities. Mitigation actions are included as definite and are performed on a timely basis in advance of the earliest need for contingent actions.

7. Each risk is evaluated for exposure.

8. There are quantified value assessments for the project. There is a commitment to measure the value that is realized after the project. There is a value-based rank-ordering of system components, provided as input to version planning.

9. There is at least some degree of incrementalism built into the project plan. Some or all of the versions are actually delivered to stakeholders or are pseudo-delivered (representing all steps included up to but not including actual delivery). Time and effort and relative-size information is captured for each version completed, and used as a mid-to-late project closure metric.

If your organization can pass at least the first six of these tests, risk management is a factor in your projects and is serving you well. If not, you still have work to do.

If you can't pass any of these tests, then we have to conclude that although your organization may talk a good game about risk management, it isn't actually doing any. Don't be too hard on yourself about this; most of our industry pays more lip service to risk management than it actually performs. But don't be too easy on yourself either. The easy assertion, "Of course we're doing risk management," in the absence of any objective evidence, is part of the problem. It lets you feel good in the short term but provides no long-term protection.

Getting past this glib assertion is the first step in making risk management work for you. It's the first step in growing up.

APPENDIX A

THE ETHICS OF BELIEF, PART 1

William Kingdon Clifford

A shipowner was about to send to sea an emigrant-ship. He knew that she was old, and not overwell built at the first; that she had seen many seas and climes, and often had needed repairs. Doubts had been suggested to him that possibly she was not seaworthy. These doubts preyed upon his mind, and made him unhappy; he thought that perhaps he ought to have her thoroughly overhauled and refitted, even though this should put him at great expense. Before the ship sailed, however, he succeeded in overcoming these melancholy reflections. He said to himself that she had gone safely through so many voyages and weathered so many storms that it was idle to suppose she would not come safely home from this trip also. He would put his trust in Providence, which could hardly fail to protect all these unhappy families that were leaving their fatherland to seek for better times elsewhere. He would dismiss from his mind all ungenerous suspicions about the honesty of builders and contractors. In such ways he acquired a sincere and comfortable conviction that his vessel was thoroughly safe and seaworthy; he watched her departure with a light heart, and benevolent wishes for the success of the exiles in their strange new home that was to be; and he got his insurance-money when she went down in mid-ocean and told no tales.

What shall we say of him? Surely this, that he was verily guilty of the death of those men. It is admitted that he did sincerely believe in the soundness of his ship; but the sincerity of his conviction can in no wise help him, because he had no right to believe on such evidence as was before him. He had acquired his belief not by honestly earning it in patient investigation, but by stifling his doubts. And although in the end he may have felt so sure about it that he could not think otherwise, yet inasmuch as he had knowingly and willingly worked himself into that frame of mind, he must be held responsible for it.

Let us alter the case a little, and suppose that the ship was not unsound after all; that she made her voyage safely, and many others after it. Will that diminish the guilt of her owner? Not one jot. When an action is once done, it is right or wrong for ever; no accidental failure of its good or evil fruits can possibly alter that. The man would not have been innocent, he would only have been not found out. The question of right or wrong has to do with the origin of his belief, not the matter of it; not what it was, but how he got it; not whether it turned out to be true or false, but whether he had a right to believe on such evidence as was before him.

There was once an island in which some of the inhabitants professed a religion teaching neither the doctrine of original sin nor that of eternal punishment. A suspicion got abroad that the professors of this religion had made use of unfair means to get their doctrines taught to children. They were accused of wresting the laws of their country in such a way as to remove children from the care of their natural and legal guardians; and even of stealing them away and keeping them concealed from their friends and relations. A certain number of men formed themselves into a society for the purpose of agitating the public about this matter. They published grave accusations against against individual citizens of the highest position and character, and did all in their power to injure these citizens in their exercise of their professions. So great was the noise they made, that a Commission was appointed to investigate the facts; but after the Commission had carefully inquired into all the evidence that could be got, it appeared that the accused were innocent. Not only had they been accused of insufficient evidence, but the evidence of their innocence was such as the agitators might easily have obtained, if they had attempted a fair inquiry. After these disclosures the inhabitants of that country looked upon the members of the agitating society, not only as persons whose judgment was to be distrusted, but also as no longer to be counted honourable men. For although they had sincerely and conscientiously believed in the charges they had made, yet they had no right to believe on such evidence as was before them. Their sincere convictions, instead of being honestly earned by patient inquiring, were stolen by listening to the voice of prejudice and passion.

Let us vary this case also, and suppose, other things remaining as before, that a still more accurate investigation proved the accused to have been really guilty. Would this make any difference in the guilt of the accusers? Clearly not; the question is not whether their belief was true or false, but whether they entertained it on wrong grounds. They would no doubt say, "Now you see that we were right after all; next time perhaps you will believe us." And they might be believed, but they would not thereby become honourable men. They would not be innocent, they would only be not found out. Every one of them, if he chose to examine himself *in foro conscientiae,* would know that he had acquired and nourished a belief, when he had no right to believe on such evidence as was before him; and therein he would know that he had done a wrong thing.

It may be said, however, that in both these supposed cases it is not the belief which is judged to be wrong, but the action following upon it. The shipowner might say, "I am perfectly certain that my ship is sound, but still I feel it my duty to have her examined, before trusting the lives of so many people to her." And it might be said to the agitator, "However convinced you were of the justice of your cause and the truth of your convictions, you ought not to have made a public attack upon any man's character until you had examined the evidence on both sides with the utmost patience and care."

In the first place, let us admit that, so far as it goes, this view of the case is right and necessary; right, because even when a man's belief is so fixed that he cannot think otherwise, he still has a choice in the action suggested by it, and so cannot escape the duty of investigating on the ground of the strength of his convictions; and necessary, because those who are not yet capable of controlling their feelings and thoughts must have a plain rule dealing with overt acts.

But this being premised as necessary, it becomes clear that it is not sufficient, and that our previous judgment is required to supplement it. For it is not possible so to sever the belief from the action it suggests as to condemn the one without condemning the other. No man holding a strong belief on one side of a question, or even wishing to hold a belief on one side, can investigate it with such fairness and completeness as if he were really in doubt and unbiased; so that the existence of a belief not founded on fair inquiry unfits a man for the performance of this necessary duty.

Nor is it that truly a belief at all which has not some influence upon the actions of him who holds it. He who truly believes that which prompts him to an action has looked upon the action to lust after it, he has committed it already in his heart. If a belief is not realized immediately in open deeds, it is stored up for the guidance of the future. It goes to make a part of that aggregate of beliefs which is the link between sensation and action at every moment of all our lives, and which is so organized and compacted together that no part of it can be isolated from the rest, but every new addition modifies the structure of the whole. No real belief, however trifling and fragmentary it may seem, is ever truly insignificant; it prepares us to receive more of its like, confirms those which resembled it before, and weakens others; and so gradually it lays a stealthy train in our inmost thoughts, which may someday explode into overt action, and leave its stamp upon our character forever.

And no one man's belief is in any case a private matter which concerns himself alone. Our lives are guided by that general conception of the course of things which has been created by society for social purposes. Our words, our phrases, our forms and processes and modes of thought, are common property, fashioned and perfected from age to age; an heirloom which every succeeding generation inherits as a precious deposit and a sacred trust to be handed on to the next one, not unchanged but enlarged and purified, with some clear marks of its proper handiwork. Into this, for good or ill, is woven every belief of every man who has speech of his fellows. An awful privilege, and an awful responsibility, that we should help to create the world in which posterity will live.

In the two supposed cases which have been considered, it has been judged wrong to believe on insufficient evidence, or to nourish belief by suppressing doubts and avoiding investigation. The reason of this judgment is not far to seek: it is that in both these cases the belief held by one man was of great importance to other men. But forasmuch as no belief held by one man, however seemingly trivial the belief, and however obscure the believer, is ever actually insignificant or without its effect on the fate of mankind, we have no choice but to extend our judgment to all cases of belief whatever. Belief, that sacred faculty which prompts the decisions of our will, and knits into harmonious working all the compacted energies of our being, is ours not for ourselves but for humanity. It is rightly used on truths which have been established by long experience and waiting toil, and which have stood in the fierce light of free and fearless questioning. Then it helps to bind men together, and to strengthen and direct their common action. It is desecrated when given to unproved and unquestioned statements, for the solace and private pleasure of the believer; to add a tinsel splendour to the plain straight road of our life and display a bright mirage beyond it; or even to drown the common sorrows of our kind by a self-deception which allows them not only to cast down, but also to degrade us. Whoso would deserve well of his fellows in this matter will guard the purity of his beliefs with a very fanaticism of jealous care, lest at any time it should rest on an unworthy object, and catch a stain which can never be wiped away.

It is not only the leader of men, statesmen, philosopher, or poet, that owes this bounden duty to mankind. Every rustic who delivers in the village alehouse his slow, infrequent sentences, may help to kill or keep alive the fatal superstitions which clog his race. Every hard-worked wife of an artisan may transmit to her children beliefs which shall knit society together, or rend it in pieces. No simplicity of mind, no obscurity of station, can escape the universal duty of questioning all that we believe.

It is true that this duty is a hard one, and the doubt which comes out of it is often a very bitter thing. It leaves us bare and powerless where we thought that we were safe and strong. To know all about anything is to know how to deal with it under all circumstances. We feel much happier and more secure when we think we know precisely what to do, no matter what happens, then when we have lost our way and do not know where to turn. And if we have supposed ourselves to know all about anything, and to be capable of doing what is fit in regard to it, we naturally do not like to find that we are really ignorant and powerless, that we have to begin again at the beginning, and try to learn what the thing is and how it is to be dealt with—if indeed anything can be learnt about it. It is the sense of power attached to a sense of knowledge that makes men desirous of believing, and afraid of doubting.

This sense of power is the highest and best of pleasures when the belief on which it is founded is a true belief, and has been fairly earned by investigation. For then we may justly feel that it is common property, and hold good for others as well as for ourselves. Then we may be glad, not that I have learned secrets by which I am safer and stronger, but that we men have got mastery over more of the world; and we shall be strong, not for ourselves but in the name of Man and his strength. But if the belief has been accepted on insufficient evidence, the pleasure is a stolen one. Not only does it deceive ourselves by giving us a sense of power which we do not really possess, but it is sinful, because it is stolen in defiance of our duty to mankind. That duty is to guard ourselves from such beliefs as from pestilence, which may shortly master our own body and then spread to the rest of the town. What would be thought of one who, for the sake of a sweet fruit, should deliberately run the risk of delivering a plague upon his family and his neighbours?

And, as in other such cases, it is not the risk only which has to be considered; for a bad action is always bad at the time when it is done, no matter what happens afterwards. Every time we let ourselves believe for unworthy reasons, we weaken our powers of self-control, of doubting, of judicially and fairly weighing evidence. We all suffer severely enough from the maintenance and support of false beliefs and the fatally wrong actions which they lead to, and the evil born when one such belief is entertained is great and wide. But a greater and wider evil arises when the credulous character is maintained and supported, when a habit of believing for unworthy reasons is fostered and made permanent. If I steal money from any person, there may be no harm done from the mere transfer of possession; he may not feel the loss, or it may prevent him from using the money badly. But I cannot help doing this great wrong towards Man, that I make myself dishonest. What hurts society is not that it should lose its property, but that it should become a den of thieves, for then it must cease to be society. This is why we ought not to do evil, that good may come; for at any rate this great evil has come, that we have done evil and are made wicked thereby. In like manner, if I let myself believe anything on insufficient evidence, there may be no great harm done by the mere belief; it may be true after all, or I may never have occasion to exhibit it in outward acts. But I cannot help doing this great wrong towards Man, that I make myself credulous. The danger to society is not merely that it should believe wrong things, though that is great enough; but that it should become credulous, and lose the habit of testing things and inquiring into them; for then it must sink back into savagery.

The harm which is done by credulity in a man is not confined to the fostering of a credulous character in others, and consequent support of false beliefs. Habitual want of care about what I believe leads to habitual want of care in others about the truth of what is told to me. Men speak the truth of one another when each reveres the truth in his own mind and in the other's mind; but how shall my friend revere the truth in my mind when I myself am careless about it, when I believe things because I want to believe them, and because they are comforting and pleasant? Will he not learn to cry, "Peace," to me, when there is no peace? By such a course I shall surround myself with a thick atmosphere of falsehood and fraud, and in that I must live. It may matter little to me, in my cloud-castle of sweet illusions and darling lies; but it matters much to Man that I have made my neighbours ready to deceive. The credulous man is father to the liar and the cheat; he lives in the bosom of this his family, and it is no marvel if he should become even as they are. So closely are our duties knit together, that whoso shall keep the whole law, and yet offend in one point, he is guilty of all.

To sum up: it is wrong always, everywhere, and for anyone, to believe anything upon insufficient evidence.

If a man, holding a belief which he was taught in childhood or persuaded of afterwards, keeps down and pushes away any doubts which arise about it in his mind, purposely avoids the reading of books and the company of men that call into question or discuss it, and regards as impious those questions which cannot easily be asked without disturbing it—the life of that man is one long sin against mankind.

If this judgment seems harsh when applied to those simple souls who have never known better, who have been brought up from the cradle with a horror of doubt, and taught that their eternal welfare depends on what they believe, then it leads to the very serious question, Who hath made Israel to sin?

It may be permitted me to fortify this judgment with the sentence of Milton—

> A man may be a heretic in the truth; and if he believe things only because his pastor says so, or the assembly so determine, without knowing other reason, though his belief be true, yet the very truth he holds becomes his heresy.[1]

And with this famous aphorism of Coleridge—

> He who begins by loving Christianity better than Truth, will proceed by loving his own sect or Church better than Christianity, and end loving himself better than all.[2]

Inquiry into the evidence of a doctrine is not to be made once for all, and then taken as finally settled. It is never lawful to stifle a doubt; for either it can be honestly answered by means of the inquiry already made, or else it proves that the inquiry was not complete.

"But," says one, "I am a busy man; I have no time for the long course of study which would be necessary to make me in any degree a competent judge of certain questions, or even able to understand the nature of the arguments."

Then he should have no time to believe.

---

[1] John Milton, *Areopagitica*, 1643.
[2] Samuel Taylor Coleridge, *Aids to Reflection*, 1825.

APPENDIX B

RISK TEMPLATE

On the following page is a proposed risk template. We are not asking you to fill in forms and manage risks by moving paper, but we want you to consider the set of information you will need to identify, assess, monitor, and reassess risks. We also want you to consider what you need to collect to build a useful risk repository, a database of past risks and their actual outcomes for use in future risk identification and assessment. Nobody's data is better than your own.

Risk Control Form

Risk Discovery and Assessment:

Short name:	Risk control number:
Originator:	Discovery date:

Description:

Probability:	Risk diagram(s) attached: [ ]
Potential cost:	Potential delay:

Selected risk materialization indicator:

Risk Planning:

Class of risk: Requires mitigation   [ ]
                 Requires contingency   [ ]
                 Accepted (no plan needed)   [ ]

Mitigation actions required (prior to materialization):

Contingency actions required (upon materialization):

Reassessment Log:

Date	Description of Change

Final Disposition:

Did risk materialize?

If yes, actual cost: ; and delay:

Comments on effectiveness of mitigation and contingency planning:

REFERENCES

Recommended Articles

Charette, Robert N. "The New Risk Management." *Cutter Consortium Executive Report, Business-IT Strategies Advisory Service,* Vol. 3, No. 9 (2000).

A 35-page treatise by the Father of RM for software.

Fairley, Richard. "Risk Management for Software Projects." *IEEE Software,* Vol. 11, No. 3 (May 1994), pp. 57–67.

The best ten-page introduction to the topic.

IEEE Computer Society. "Managing Risk." *IEEE Software,* Vol. 14, No. 3 (May/June 1997).

Risk is the theme for the entire issue.

Keen, Peter G.W. "Information Systems and Organizational Change." *Communications of the ACM,* Vol. 24, No. 1 (January 1981), pp. 24–33.

For those of you wanting to focus only on technical risk, a primer on customer/organizational risk. For every implementation, expect at least one counter-implementation. An oldie, but a goodie!

U.S. General Accounting Office. "New Denver Airport: Impact of the Delayed Baggage System," GAO Report GAO/RCED-95-35BR (October 1994).

Carry-on.

Recommended Books

Charette, Robert N. *Software Engineering Risk Analysis and Management.* New York: McGraw-Hill, 1989.

Not the easiest read, but the most detailed treatment. Really interesting stuff, once you get going.

DeMarco, Tom. *The Deadline: A Novel About Project Management.* New York: Dorset House Publishing, 1997.

A project management novel . . . yes, a novel . . . with a real risk: If the manager can't bring in the project, he will die.

Goldratt, Eliyahu M. *Critical Chain.* Great Barrington, Mass.: The North River Press, 1997.

An amazing novel about project management exploring why projects are always late, and what we should do about the problem. We don't know if we agree entirely, but the book's a mind-boggler just the same. It will make you rethink everything.

Grey, Stephen. *Practical Risk Assessment for Project Management.* Chichester, England: John Wiley & Sons, 1995.

A Brit's views on RM—Grey is from ICL, UK. Straightforward, this book discusses software support for RM as well as risk assessment. It uses the Palisade Corporation's software package *@RISK* for its examples.

Hall, Elaine M. *Managing Risk: Methods for Software Systems Development.* Reading, Mass.: Addison-Wesley, 1998.

> Another solid primer on software risk. This book describes in detail the stages of organizational maturity in the context of RM.

Jones, Capers. *Assessment and Control of Software Risks.* Englewood Cliffs, N.J.: PTR Prentice Hall, 1994.

> Interesting coverage of the most common risks by system type. Stun your boss with amazing statistics!

McConnell, Steve. *Rapid Development: Taming Wild Software Schedules.* Redmond, Wash.: Microsoft Press, 1996.

> Six-hundred-fifty pages of readable, sensible advice. Includes an entire chapter on risk management, and ties RM cleanly to the rapid development theme.

Wideman, R. Max, ed. *Project & Program Risk Management: A Guide to Managing Project Risks and Opportunities.* Newton Square, Penn.: Project Management Institute, 1992.

> The folks at PMI have integrated RM into PMBOK— their project management body of knowledge. This is the risk guide in the PMI nine-volume series.

Recommended Websites

Cutter Consortium. Risk Management Intelligence Network: http://www.cutter.com/risk/index.html

> Directed by Bob Charette, this pay site has must-read articles, highly informative Q&A sessions, and ongoing discussion groups.

Department of the Air Force, Software Technology Support Center. "Guidelines for Successful Acquisition and Management of Software-Intensive Systems," Version 3.0 (May 2000): http://www.stsc.hill.af.mil/resources/tech_docs/gsam3.html

> About much more than just risk management, this 14-chapter report does a very good job of treating the topic, focusing Chapter 6 exclusively on RM. The whole report (or part) is free for the download. . . . U.S. tax dollars at work, and worth it.

Department of Defense. Reports citing RM from the DoD Software Acquisition Best Practices Initiative, Software Program Managers Network (SPMN): http://www.spmn.com

> The SPMN initiative, which is run by the U.S. Navy for the DoD, has produced many interesting (free) hand-outs covering risk management, among other topics. Risk Radar, an RM tool, is free for the download.

IEEE Std. 1540-2001, "IEEE Standard for Software Life Cycle Processes—Risk Management." Los Alamitos, Calif.: IEEE Computer Society Press, 2001: http://www.ieee.org

> The accepted process standard from the IEEE.

Software Engineering Institute. "Taxonomy Based Risk Identification," Report No. SEI.93-TR-006: http://www.sei.cmu.edu/publications/documents/93.reports/93.tr.006.html

> This report includes the SEI risk taxonomy; a risk-identification starter kit of some 194 questions.

Related References

Brainstorming

de Bono, Edward. *Lateral Thinking: Creativity Step by Step.* New York: Perennial, Harper & Row, 1990.

> The classic from the Father of Brainstorming.

_____. *Six Thinking Hats*. Boston: Little Brown & Co., 1999.

Who needs just stereoscopic vision? Six ways to look
at things.

von Oech, Roger. *A Whack on the Side of the Head: How You
Can Be More Creative*. New York: Warner Books, 1998.

Mental calisthenics for creativity.

Incrementalism

Beck, Kent. *Extreme Programming Explained: Embrace Change*.
Reading, Mass.: Addison-Wesley, 2000.

If you have not read about XP or the other agile
methodologies, start here.

_____, and Martin Fowler. *Planning Extreme Programming*.
Reading, Mass.: Addison-Wesley, 2001.

When viewed as a set of RM strategies, XP makes all
kinds of sense. The two-week planning and delivery
cycle determined by the customer is a built-in risk-mitigation strategy with customer-defined value and is
designed to prevent late delivery. As Beck and Fowler
state on page 18, "A good customer is willing to accept
the ultimate responsibility for the success or failure of
the project." Can that happen where you work?

Gilb, Tom. *Principles of Software Engineering Management,* ed.
Susannah Finzi. Wokingham, England: Addison-Wesley, 1988.

Gilb is one of the strongest, and earliest, advocates for
incremental development, what he calls "evolutionary
delivery."

Postmortems

Collier, Bonnie, Tom DeMarco, and Peter Fearey. "A Defined Process for Project Postmortem Review." *IEEE Software,* Vol. 13, No. 4 (July 1996), pp. 65–72.

> Just as the title of the article indicates, a *defined process* is what is needed—no reminiscing!

Kerth, Norman L. *Project Retrospectives: A Handbook for Team Reviews.* New York: Dorset House Publishing, 2001.

> This focused little book will help you get the feedback loop in place so you can learn how to do better in the future.

Real-World Tales

Bernstein, Peter L. *Against the Gods: The Remarkable Story of Risk.* New York: John Wiley & Sons, 1996.

> This book tells the story of a group of thinkers who showed the world how to understand and measure risk, noting on page 1 that "the revolutionary idea that defines the boundary between modern times and the past is the mastery of risk. . . ."

Bridges, William. *Managing Transitions: Making the Most of Change.* Reading, Mass.: Perseus Books, 1991.

> Why getting people to change their ways is so darned hard—*hint: It is always emotional*—and what you can do to help the change happen.

Petroski, Henry. *To Engineer Is Human: The Role of Failure in Successful Design.* New York: Vintage Books, 1992.

> A professor in the Civil and Environmental Engineering Department at Duke University, Petroski writes about how real engineers deal to great advantage with real risk. A true classic, originally published in 1985.

Rawnsley, Judith H. *Total Risk: Nick Leeson and the Fall of Barings Bank*. New York: HarperBusiness, 1995.

> How does a 28-year-old trader take down a mighty financial institution? One bad bet after another, and nobody bothering to watch! A tangible result of the absence of RM. You just can't make this stuff up.

U.S. Marine Corps Staff. *Warfighting: The U.S. Marine Corps Book of Strategy*. New York: Currency Doubleday, 1994.

> What? A book on fighting wars? Yes, this terrific little book is both about fighting wars and succeeding at software projects. And yes, it is absolutely relevant to you.

Vaughan, Karen. *The Challenger Launch Decision: Risky Technology, Culture, and Deviance at NASA*. Chicago: University of Chicago Press, 1996.

> The public record says that the Space Shuttle *Challenger* was lost because of political and economic pressure overwhelming reasonable risk management. This book, a serious and scholarly work, proposes something much more subtle, and much more worrisome for all organizations.

Root Cause Analysis

Andersen, Bjorn, ed. *Root Cause Analysis: Simplified Tools and Techniques*. Milwaukee: American Society for Quality, 1999.

> A highly rated treatment of the subject.

Gano, Dean. *Apollo Root Cause Analysis: A New Way of Thinking*, ed. Vicki E. Lee. Yakima, Wash.: Apollonian Publications, 1999.

> Another very popular text on root cause analysis.

Goal/QPC. "Hoshin Planning Research Report." Salem, N.H.: Goal/QPC, 1989.

> See especially Chapter 4, "Affinity Diagrams and the KJ Method."

Shiba, Shoji, Alan Graham, and David Walden. *A New American TQM*. Portland, Oreg.: Productivity Press, 1993.

> Root cause analysis, this time in the context of Total Quality Management.

WinWin Spiral Model

Boehm, Barry W., and Hoh In. "Identifying Quality-Requirements Conflicts." *IEEE Software,* Vol. 13, No. 2 (March 1996), pp. 25–35.

> An interesting introduction. For substantive information on the WinWin Spiral Model, go to the University of Southern California's Website: http://sunset.usc.edu/research/WINWIN/winwinspiral.html

INDEX

The Deadline

A Novel About Project Management

by Tom DeMarco

ISBN: 0-932633-39-0 ©1997 320 pages softcover
$30.95 (includes $6.00 for UPS in US)*

Winner of a Software Development Productivity Award

From prolific and influential consultant and author Tom DeMarco comes a project management novel that vividly illustrates the principles—and the outright *absurdities*—that affect the productivity of a software development team.

With his trademark wit set free in the novel format, DeMarco centers the plot around the development of six software products. Mr. Tompkins, a manager downsized from a giant telecommunications company, divides the huge staff of developers at his disposal into eighteen teams—three for each of the software products. The teams are different sizes and use different methods, and they compete

against each other and against an *impossible* deadline.

With these teams—and with the help of numerous "fictionalized" consultants who come to his aid—Tompkins tests the project management principles he has gathered over a lifetime. Each chapter closes with journal entries that form the core of the eye-opening approaches to management illustrated in this entertaining novel.

"Here's a management book which is just plain fun to read. *The Deadline* is an innovative and entertaining story with insightful business principles for team-based project management at the end of each chapter."
—John Sculley

"entertaining—and simultaneously instructive. . . . many valuable techniques."
—**Warren Keuffel,** *Software Development*

"On content, Tom has produced a gem. . . . a lot of good common sense coupled with a nice seasoning of wisdom. The way the stories are packaged, the messages are easy to grasp and remember. . . . All in all, this is a relaxing and informative read."
—Watts S. Humphrey
Fellow, Software Engineering Institute

"Tom DeMarco once again gleefully peels away the onion layers of management issues with a humanity and insight that translate as easily into corporate general management as they do into the management of software projects and teams." **—Bruce Taylor**
Founding Publisher, *ImagingWorld*

"offers a balanced approach to project management. The author rightly pinpoints people as the essential foundation of all successful projects." **—Quality Digest**

Read more about THE DEADLINE *at www.dorsethouse.com/books/dl.html*

Order Today! • (800) 342-6657 • (212) 620-4053 • fax (212) 727-1044
Phone, fax, or mail with credit card information, check, or money order. *Prices subject to change without notice.
DORSET HOUSE PUBLISHING 353 WEST 12TH STREET NEW YORK, NEW YORK 10014 USA
info@dorsethouse.com • www.dorsethouse.com